# Enticing Environments

## for People Under Three

Laura Wilhelm, EdD

Gryphon House
www.gryphonhouse.com

## BULK PURCHASE

Gryphon House books are available for special premiums and sales promotions as well as for fund-raising use. Special editions or book excerpts also can be created to specifications. For details, call 800.638.0928.

## DISCLAIMER

Gryphon House, Inc., cannot be held responsible for damage, mishap, or injury incurred during the use of or because of activities in this book. Appropriate and reasonable caution and adult supervision of children involved in activities and corresponding to the age and capability of each child involved are recommended at all times. Do not leave children unattended at any time. Observe safety and caution at all times.

# Table of Contents

# Introduction

Classroom learning environments can have a huge impact on the ways children learn, develop skills, gain confidence, and make connections. Even for very young children—infants, toddlers, and two-year-olds—environments help shape their learning. In this book, we will explore aspects of inviting, interesting, and intriguing environments and discuss ways to develop your classroom to create a space that nurtures, supports, and challenges the people under three in your care.

- ○ We'll consider colors, sounds, smells, furniture placement, lighting, and textures.

- ○ We'll look at grouping by age and providing age-appropriate routines.

- ○ We'll consider ways to support language and physical, emotional, and cognitive development.

Throughout, I've included photos taken in real spaces inhabited by people under three. These ideas are, for the most part, easy to do with low-cost materials and a little creativity. (It also helps to know someone who is handy with tools.) I hope they will inspire you to try out some of the ideas in your own classroom space.

Research (and experience) tells us that a classroom space that meets the needs of its inhabitants is a place where children and the adults who care for them can thrive. I hope that the ideas and information shared in this book will inspire you and enrich your work with the children you care for.

# CHAPTER 1

## The Brilliance of Babies, Toddlers, and Twos

Babies are brilliant. If you don't believe it, spend just a few minutes watching a very young child explore a novel object. You can almost see the little wheels turning in her mind. A person under three years old has a mountain of work ahead of her. In just a matter of months, she will begin to figure out how her body works: how to grasp, to roll over, and then to sit, stand, climb, and run!

Even newborn babies display impressive capabilities and curiosity as they respond to caregivers and learn to elicit responses from the ever-expanding world around them.

Babies are born scientists. They are prewired for curiosity and discovery. We can see that they are beginning to build a concept of themselves when they start to play with the "baby in the mirror." It's evident that they are building an understanding of the world beyond their own bodies when they register surprise at the unexpected. We don't have to wonder whether they are ready to learn something new—when they are ready to try out a new skill, they simply do it! Our job is to pay careful attention and use their cues to help us provide safe, appropriate environments where they can thrive. Strive to see babies as intently as they see us.

Elinor Goldschmied was an educator who worked with orphaned babies who were kept in group care during and after World War II. To convey her deep respect for babies, she used the term "people under three"—not "little ones," which can sound

condescending, or even *infants*, which can sound distant like medical terminology. At the time, people thought that babies were cute but not very capable. Many thought they interacted with the world only to cry, sleep, and eat. Researchers (even as recently as the 1980s!) thought that, due to immature pain receptors, babies could not really experience pain. Parents were told, "Oh, it doesn't really hurt to draw blood from the bottom of a newborn's foot." Science is now teaching us that babies do feel pain, much like adults do. Babies are much more aware and interactive than people have assumed—something that Goldschmied understood. Today, researchers are finding new ways to demonstrate what babies already know and how they are continually learning.

In some ways, we've underestimated babies' capabilities. Repeated altruism studies (Warneken and Tomasello, 2006; Hu, Li, Jia, and Xie, 2016; Barragan, Brooks, and Meltzoff, 2020) have demonstrated that toddlers as young as fifteen months will help others, even when there's no reward for themselves and even when they have to overcome obstacles to help another person. Young children are not only capable; they will go out of their way to be helpful, especially when they have had previous interactions with the person who needs their help.

We also overestimate young children. A toddler may demonstrate an interest in numeracy, arranging objects one by one. Although this play is laying the foundation for later arithmetic, this behavior does not mean the child is ready for math problems. Despite the commercials you may have seen featuring very young children recognizing letter patterns and imitating reading-like behaviors, babies do not need to learn to read—not yet. The time invested in teaching babies these academic-looking tricks would be much better spent playing with them.

By following their lead and facilitating their discoveries, we can help babies build on their current level of understanding. Children will show us what they need, if we pay attention; their every behavior is communicating information. Babies need to be nurtured and given lots of interesting experiences, which build a strong foundation for the academic instruction that will come later. The first years are a time for exploration and learning with all the senses. When we closely observe spontaneous play, we can see a child's current understanding and can plan ways to present new challenges.

Pediatrician T. Berry Brazelton and his colleagues created an instrument called the *Neonatal Behavioral Assessment Scale* (NBAS) to showcase the abilities of newborns. The scale teaches families that their newborns are already learning and using inborn reflexes. For example, from the very first day of life, babies show preference for familiar voices. If you hold a newborn baby in your arms and have a parent speak on one side and a stranger speak on the other, the baby will turn toward the parent. Cells in the brain called *mirror neurons* allow babies to imitate the facial expressions of people around them. For example, even brand-new babies can imitate tongue thrusts. If you stick your tongue out at a baby a few times, she will slowly start sticking her tongue back out at you! (Try it with the child of friends. They might wonder about you, but they will be impressed with their newborn's skills.) Babies can identify their own mothers' milk by smell from the day they are born. They can track a small red ball with their eyes. And they will make reflexive stepping motions when you hold them upright. When parents are shown these capabilities, they begin to see their baby as a person who knows them already. We don't have to wait years to begin teaching them; babies are already learning from day one. As humans, we are programmed to view our own children as very special. Our preference helps us protect them. The NBAS helps us see them as learners as well.

Yes, reading to young children is important for their development, but so are singing, dancing, talking, and playing. Objects in the environment present opportunities for learning. Very young children learn through all their senses:

touch, taste, smell, sight, and sound. They are drawn to interesting textures, such as woven baskets and wooden blocks. After the age of six months, when babies are introduced to solid food, allowing them to explore it with their fingers combines nutrition with lessons about taste, texture, smell, and sound. Toddlers can identify vegetables by taste, color, and shape as they select what to eat next.

Babies respond to our singing—even when we sing badly. They love laughter, the noises they make with their own voices, kicking, and banging objects. When babies babble, they take turns, pause, and gesture at the same rate as adults who are having a conversation. Their voices rise in pitch before a pause to indicate questions, and at other times, they can sound very emphatic. Babies' babbling mimics the languages that they hear used most often.

Babies need freedom of movement to explore the world and to develop their muscles. While playing indoors and outside, they need to be able to push up, roll over, squirm, and kick. They need time on the floor on their tummies to strengthen the muscles in their arms, necks, and shoulders by pushing up. They will use these muscles later for crawling. They need time on their backs to relax, stretch, and kick. Once they can roll over, they'll start to find ways to scoot their bodies toward interesting objects. They cannot do any of these things when they're strapped into the seat of a bouncer or swing.

Some babies do love to be in those containers, but they should always be taken out of them within 20 minutes because the containers limit babies' range of motion and muscle development. So-called "walkers" don't teach babies how to walk, because babies in them aren't supporting their own weight. Very young children need lots of opportunities to pull up to a standing position and to cruise along pieces of furniture as practice for later walking.

## Enticing, Engaging Environments

Appropriate environments are part of the educational curriculum for our youngest citizens. Carefully planned environments nurture curiosity and invite children to explore and experiment with their own ideas. When babies crawl on the floor, little

fingers love to try to fit into a tiny knothole in the floorboard. Crawlers are drawn to discover interesting textures such as woven mats, smooth tile floors, rubber pads, and soft carpets. Toddlers become obsessed with walking and running as soon as they are able. They love toys that they can push and pull, and they enjoy climbing steps or stairs. Two-year-olds can be very creative and may begin to create storylines to narrate their play with blocks and puppets. For example, as he entered our school each morning, a two-year-old made a ritual of turning two fabric birds with wire legs facedown on the table as he walked past my office. After a few days, his mom explained his reason: "So they could eat."

Big eyes are drawn to beautiful patterns displayed at the child's eye level. To see for yourself what the children are seeing, get down on the floor. Observe what is visible near your ankle height. What do you notice? Do you see table legs, shoes, and shelving? Is there anything interesting that a baby might want to scoot, roll, crawl, or toddle over to investigate? On your knees, look at the room from your normal elbow height to replicate the view when babies are being cuddled in a lap. How does the room look different from here? Is there artwork on the walls? Do you see mobiles made of interesting items? Stand and examine what is visible at your shoulder height when babies are lifted or carried. Can you see outside through a window? Do you notice a loft to explore or a mobile to gaze at?

## Display Beauty

Babies, toddlers, and twos appreciate beautiful design and calming interiors just like adults. Rooms should feature beautiful artwork, have blank spaces where eyes can rest, windows to see outdoors, and mirrors to reflect light and allow babies to see their own and others' faces. Paint the walls in comforting colors that fade into the background, so that the focus of the classroom is on children's work and not the walls. Artwork should be lovely to look at; display children's art projects respectfully. For example, if children have explored making marks on large sheets of paper, trim the edges evenly rather than just ripping the paper off the roll. Take a little extra time to tape paintings and drawings into empty picture frames or mats, and hang them on the walls where the children can see them. Consider using open-topped Plexiglas frames, which will allow you to change out photos and artwork from time to time. You can safely display the images near the floor where young children can view them up close.

## Offer Places and Things to Explore

An open floor plan with a clear line of sight allows for supervision by sight and sound at all times, which is necessary for safety. Babies need open floor space where they can move, and they need opportunities to explore the environment safely. In an area for babies, provide rugs and mats that have soft and inviting textures where they can lie on their backs or tummies, protected from mobile children by shelves or gates. Provide a variety of easy-to-clean surfaces for rolling, scooting, and crawling, such as linoleum, wood, tile, or vinyl flooring—especially in the feeding, diapering, sensory, and art-exploration areas. You can add variety and interest with temporary texture additions to your classroom floor. Try duct-taping squares of burlap, cotton fabric, and even contact paper turned sticky side up for the children to check out. Babies love to touch their families' and friends' photos when displayed under clear contact paper on a smooth floor.

Give babies low, sturdy shelves to pull up on and crawl through. Provide interesting things to look at and move toward, such as unbreakable mirrors, artwork, open space, plants, windows, photographs, and mobiles. Offer safe things to grasp, such as balls made of rolled socks, yarn, cloth, or wicker; pretty handkerchiefs or small scarves; sponges; lightweight kitchen utensils; soft blocks; and rope lights. Provide toys, books, and materials to explore. Outdoors, babies enjoy the textures of grass,

sidewalks, mats, blankets, sand, and dirt. Create shady areas with books, blankets, and toys to explore.

Toddlers want to be upright whenever possible. This desire is so strong that parents sometimes find their toddlers asleep in their cribs upright and holding onto the railings. Toddlers are excited to practice their new walking skills, but these are still developing, so provide soft carpets as a safe place to land. Lay out rugs and mats with soft and inviting textures, which can be rearranged and do not present tripping hazards. Give toddlers large pillows to crash into for big body play.

They need wide, clear pathways between interest areas and engaging things to go look at, such as unbreakable mirrors, artwork, open space, plants, windows, photographs, and kites. Small pillows and blocks invite lifting and carrying, two favorite toddler sports. Clear containers allow toddlers to choose what they want to explore and begin to participate in cleanup by making a game of sorting toys into the bins correctly. Provide clearly marked, easily accessible containers of toys, books, and materials on low, sturdy shelves.

Toddlers like things they can carry, such as bags, boxes, and purses, and they love putting things, such as bracelets, necklaces, or blocks, inside. They love cozy spots that they can fit their bodies into. Low, sturdy shelves provide safe places to pull up and explore lovely items. Give them lockers and cubbies that they can reach so they can begin to help with putting on their own coats and shoes and putting away their work.

Offer steps and ramps where they can practice their climbing and balancing skills. Provide toys to push and pull and ride on with their feet on the floor. At the changing tables, toilets, and sinks, place sturdy steps to support the toddlers' developing self-help skills. Outdoors, provide areas with sun, shade, sand, paths for wheeled toys, plants to water, sensory play, art explorations, and loose parts to manipulate.

Two-year-olds are quickly developing their social, language, motor, and self-help skills. They need clearly defined interest areas and cozy spaces where they can play alone or with a friend. Provide shelves and containers marked with symbols to guide children in helping with cleanup, and offer easy-to-reach lockers and cubbies to support two-year-olds in putting on their own coats and shoes.

Offer interesting things for exploring perspectives, such as unbreakable mirrors, artwork, open space, plants, windows, photographs, tents, and lofts. Provide things to climb, such as steps and slides; things to push, such as shopping carts, doll strollers, and wheeled toys; and things to ride, such as pedal cars and trikes. Offer scarves, ribbons, parachutes, loose parts, capes, art materials, blocks, dolls, cars, and ramps to explore.

Add some rugs and mats with soft and inviting textures, which can be rearranged and do not present tripping hazards. Offer outdoor areas with sun, shade, sand, paths for wheeled toys, plants to water, sensory play, art, and loose parts.

## Consider the Furniture

Child-size furniture invites a feeling of accomplishment because children can help themselves independently as they actively participate in the classroom. Including chairs of a few different heights will allow each child to sit with both feet touching the floor. Consider providing child-height feeding chairs that allow crawlers, toddlers, and twos to seat themselves. This will give the adults more time to prepare food and respond to each child's hunger cues. Family-style mealtime helps caregivers get to know each child's preferences and eating style. Socializing and bonding during these sensory-rich experiences help children feel connected, seen, and nurtured.

Low, sturdy shelves give newly mobile people a place to practice pulling up, standing, and cruising along the edge. Low lofts add additional challenges with ramps, platforms, and railings. Children can practice their crawling and walking skills on these structures.

Chapter 1: The Brilliance of Babies, Toddlers, and Twos   **13**

Diapering should actually be a pleasant experience. It's an opportunity for one-to-one communication and bonding while also building a sense of teamwork and accomplishment. For young babies, a deep well in the changing table will keep them safe from rolling over or rolling off the table during diaper changes. For older babies, a changing table with stairs that can lock in place when needed and safely stow out of the way when not in use allows toddlers to actively participate in their own care. Caregivers (and their backs) will appreciate not having to repeatedly lift larger children up and down from the changing table. Wall-mounted diaper storage will keep extra diapers, wipes, clean clothes, and other essentials close at hand for efficient diaper changes. Removable seamless changing pads are easier to sanitize. Teachers report that having disposable paper rolls attached to the changing table makes cleaning and disinfecting quicker between diaper changes.

In a multi-age classroom, use shelves or a customizable gate system to allow not-yet-mobile babies to have a safe space to explore without the risk of being bumped into by busy toddlers. Clear gate panels and shelves with clear backs allow babies and toddlers to interact with each other from separated parts of the classroom. Unbreakable mirrors on shelf backs and gate panels reflect the light in the room and provide places for children to play with their reflections.

## Invite Conversations

A very important indicator of high-quality care is the quality of interactions between children and adults. Adult voices shouldn't dominate the sounds of a classroom. There should be give and take with speaking and listening, even in young infant classrooms. The pauses in our talking allow the babies to respond to us. Babies practice speech by making noises that are about the length of typical words in the languages that they hear. They quickly figure out how long to wait for other people to speak before responding with more babbling, and then they pause to listen again. They will become visibly upset if you don't respond in the expected time frame. And when they need a break from interactions, they will turn their heads away and slowly blink or yawn to let you know. Occasionally, I have observed babies giving these cues and the adults totally missing them. They'll turn the babies' faces back to continue playing. A baby may start crying out of fatigue and frustration, leaving the adult confused because she missed these signals.

When you interact with a baby, always tell her what you plan to do next so she can associate those words with their meaning. For example, never swoop a baby up from behind when you're preparing to change her diaper. Imagine yourself happily playing on the floor and suddenly you become airborne as someone picks you up from behind without warning and carries you across the room. That would be an unpleasant surprise! Instead, approach the baby from the front and say something like, "Alka, I know you're having fun playing with that ball. It's time to change your diaper. Would you like to take the ball with you? I'm going to pick you up and carry you to the changing area. Here we go!"

Babies should eat, sleep, and be diapered according to their own needs, not a predetermined schedule. Encourage babies to fall asleep when they become drowsy, feed them when they show signs of hunger, and promptly change soiled diapers in a respectful and nurturing way that teaches them that the world is a place they can trust. Observe the babies in your care, and learn to recognize their cues. Comment on what you observe. For example, say, "Heidi, I see you're rubbing your eyes. Are you feeling sleepy? I think you might need to take a nap. Would you like to get your lovie?" Or "Derek, I hear you fussing. Are you feeling hungry? I think you must be—you've been playing for a while. Let's go get something to eat." Or "Mark, it looks like your diaper is full. Let's go to the changing area and get you cleaned up."

Infant and toddler classrooms are worlds apart. It's easy to get overwhelmed by the logistics of diapering, documenting diaper checks and eating, and cleaning and sanitizing. Layer on top of that special parent requests and center initiatives. It's no wonder providers are exhausted. We have great responsibility. With every diaper change or every conversation that feels one-sided, we are actually building brains! We are teaching babies that the world is a predictable place where they can trust that certain things will happen in ways they can anticipate. Each time we make babies laugh, smile, or just feel safe, we are strengthening their neural pathways. The brain is a use-dependent organ. That means the more babies and adults use their brains, the more efficient their brains become. The opposite is also true: the more we avoid thinking, the weaker the neural pathways become. Supportive environments strengthen the amazing capabilities of very young people by providing opportunities for sensory exploration, by nurturing natural curiosity, and by keeping babies safe and healthy.

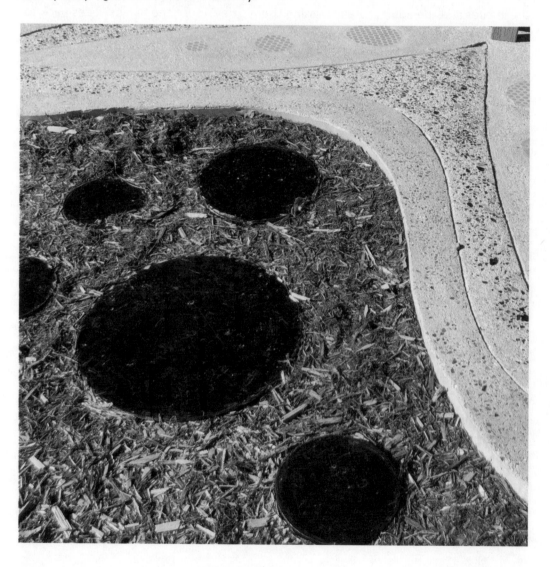

# CHAPTER 2

## The Environmental Mentor

Child-care environments play an important role in how babies, toddlers, and two-year-olds experience learning. Colors, sounds, smells, the placement of furniture, lighting, and textures all influence how people act and interact inside a classroom. As early childhood professionals continually seek better ways to help young children learn new information, we plan experiences to help them gain knowledge, practice new skills, and apply those ideas in different situations.

## Habitats and Habits

A *habitat* is a place where an organism or a community of organisms lives. Habitats include all the living and nonliving parts of the surrounding environment. Classroom habitats for people under three include living things, such as babies and toddlers, older children in the school, adult staff and families, as well as classroom pets and the bugs and squirrels on the playground. Indoor and outdoor plants, trees, bushes, and gardens are parts of the living habitat. Classroom habitats also include nonliving things, such as the furniture, rugs, walls, toys, materials, and equipment. These spaces can be peaceful, chaotic, and everything in between over the course of a single day. When habitats are generally calm and offer engaging activities, children and teachers can enjoy the time spent there and will learn more efficiently. Those who inhabit the space will experience less stress and feel more comfortable, which leaves them more intellectually available for learning.

*Habits* are learned repeated behaviors. To create a peaceful and organized environment, we need to teach and practice positive habits. The environment has an impact on the behaviors and habits of the people who spend time there, as do teacher expectations, appropriate curriculum, and even the personalities and moods of children themselves. To plan effective lessons, we need to ask questions such as the following:

- What will the children do while they are here?
- What supplies and materials do we need to occupy their time?
- How can we help them learn to treat each other with kindness and respect?

Intentional environmental planning works like having another kind of teacher in the classroom. A well-planned environment with a thoughtfully implemented curriculum provides for deeper learning and a more enjoyable experience for all the people who inhabit it.

## The 3 *I*'s: Inviting, Interesting, and Intriguing

*Inviting. Interesting. Intriguing.* These three *I*'s may sound similar at first, but each one is different when you consider them a little bit more deeply. We can *invite* a baby to notice something, then help him learn more about it. We can make the object more engaging by capturing the child's *interest* and, finally, can tap into the child's curiosity through creating deeper *intrigue* and complexity. If you have spent time with people under three (or have watched YouTube videos), you know that babies want to find out whether repeating an action causes the same response each time. By planning for deeper engagement, you can help children become more involved with classroom activities that interest them. When young children are engaged in meaningful ways in the classroom, they will be less fussy and will feel happier. Children who are focused on learning will interact more peacefully with one another.

If we want our programs to be inviting so that families and staff feel at home, we need to plan spaces that welcome them to enter. If we want environments to be interesting, we need materials that will encourage further exploration. If we want our habitats to be intriguing so that infants and toddlers follow their curiosity and engage with activities, we need to offer choices that add complexity and surprises. These three *I*'s—inviting, interesting, and intriguing—serve as a guide for planning more engaging environments inhabited by young children.

I have had the opportunity to visit the Jean Tyson Child Development Study Center at the University of Arkansas. This is a model early childhood facility that offers programs for infants, toddlers, and preschoolers. University students use the facility as a teaching laboratory, and it serves as a research facility for faculty and graduate students. The Tyson Center is a wonderful example of the three *I*'s, as the photos in this chapter will show.

## Inviting Programs

The three I's can also be applied to the center itself. Some quality child-care programs are housed in new buildings that were expressly designed for the number and ages of children who will attend. Other excellent child-care programs have been created in spaces that are decades or even centuries old and originally designed for entirely different purposes.

You get a sense of what the place is going to be like as soon as you approach the building. Think about the building's curb appeal as families approach your center. Visible signs with clear messages convey a welcoming spirit, if they explain entry procedures so that visitors know what they are supposed to do. It is less stressful for new families and visitors if they know that they are in the right place and have an idea of what they should do next.

Once inside a child-care center, a visitor's senses immediately receive messages from the environment. Smell may be the first sense engaged. Centers should smell clean but not like strong bleach, fresh but not like chemical air fresheners. Remember that many children and adults have allergies to scented air fresheners and perfumes. Good ventilation with fresh air brings positive smells into the building. Food being prepared in the kitchen or as a lesson in a classroom can make the whole building smell inviting. I've worked in centers where the staff bake bread or make popcorn each week to create a welcoming scent throughout the building.

The entry space should be visually appealing. For safety's sake, as well as for hospitality, it should be free from clutter. As humans, we are drawn to natural light from windows. If an entry lacks sufficient windows, reflective surfaces such as mirrors, white boards, and tiles can bounce light around the space.

The entry should be acoustically appealing too. Rugs, acoustic ceiling tiles, curtains, and even thin wall-to-wall carpet can dampen echoes. But take care not to absorb too much of the sound, because that will cause the place to sound muffled and feel uncomfortable. Seek a balance of easy-to-clean hard surfaces and sound-absorbing soft materials.

Colors are important because they influence our feelings and behaviors. Many people think bright primary colors are required for young children, but these colors tend to make us all feel restless. Many fast-food places use red, orange, and yellow in their dining rooms to keep people moving rather than spending a lot of time there. To help children and their families to feel at home, we should choose

home-like, comforting colors. Textures also make an entry more inviting. Look for interesting textures when selecting rugs, pots, artwork, and seating.

Live plants can improve the air quality and create a peaceful atmosphere. They also give children a chance to practice taking care of living things by helping to water, repot, and trim. If it's not possible to add live plants, artificial plants and even pictures of plants and trees will have a calming effect on the mood.

At the Jean Tyson Center, visitors are greeted by child- and adult-size chairs where they can sit to enjoy picture books from the lending library and parent resources. Natural light, homelike furniture and fabrics, and plants give the space an inviting feel. Displays explain the program's philosophy.

## Interesting Programs

A center's entryway is an excellent place to capture a child's interest and invite families into the center. Of course, there are the required bulletin boards for legal notices, sign-in areas, and reception desks. Consider adding seating so that families can comfortably adjust their bags, strollers, and coats. I once worked in a school with a big, beautiful aquarium that graced the entry with peaceful sounds

and motion but required a passionate staff member, and then a paid service, to provide upkeep. I visited a center with a bronze sculpture of children playing at the beach surrounded by sand in the entryway. Children would rush up to the table, scooping the sand with their hands and letting it slip through their fingers as they arrived each day. The family who donated this sand table and sculpture initially wanted to have a fountain, but that wasn't allowed by licensing, so they found a beautiful compromise. Another center created a lovely living-room-like space with comfortable chairs around a sand table that was used like a coffee table. Children spent a few minutes playing as their families checked in at the desk. It also served as a positive way to extend morning transition time for those children who were reluctant to allow their families to leave. Placing a flannel board with detachable pieces to arrange in the entryway can be an inviting morning routine for children to engage in as families sign them in. Another center created a coffee station for parents to stop by on their way out of the building each morning. Families saved time and money by skipping the line at the coffee shop and got a few minutes to build relationships with other parents and the staff in the front office.

Shared spaces are places within a center that are used by more than one group. We can create deeper engagement opportunities for all children, including our youngest learners, by offering activities in shared spaces that capture their attention and make them want to find out more. Shared spaces may be as different as the centers themselves. Some schools have wide hallways or pods that provide space for learning centers between the classrooms, which can be used by all of the surrounding rooms. A school that I have visited sets up projectors playing a video loop of natural environments: falling leaves, a creek, rain, or snow. This creates a magical pretending space for toddlers to interact with the rich visual imagery.

Shared spaces between classrooms make great areas for additional play centers that may not fit in the classroom. For example, children can play with grocery-store props, such as empty food boxes and shopping carts, in a store center. Natural clay on a low table creates an invitation to make a sculpture or just squeeze the clay. To make shared spaces safe for the youngest players, check for and remove choking hazards. Ensure there's nothing unstable that could fall over or that toddlers can pull down on themselves. And make sure electrical outlets have safety caps or are otherwise inaccessible.

Shared outdoor spaces can vary greatly. I have visited schools that have immaculate playgrounds that look like a shady city park or a grandparent's backyard. I recently

visited a school whose playground consisted of four parking spaces in the corner of a shopping strip. Each day, these dedicated professionals carry out all of the play equipment necessary to meet their licensing regulations and set up a playground in the parking lot. At the end of the day, they put it all away again.

For people under three, outdoor spaces need to have some shade, because their skin is thinner and more sensitive than that of adults. The spaces need fences or barriers to define the area and allow for supervision. Beach blankets are nice for nonmobile infants and for toddlers who want to relax and look at the clouds or a book. To intrigue toddlers, provide wheeled toys that they can push or ride. They especially enjoy scooping and pouring sand and water, so create a spot where they can interact with these materials. They love pretending to cook with real pots, pans and spoons, so a kitchen area would attract and hold their attention. And bring out bags or purses that they can put smaller items inside and take them out again. Two-year-olds love collecting sticks and acorns in buckets, playing with sand toys and cars, and pretending in mud kitchens. Providing the materials for these activities would fascinate them.

The Tyson Center offers shared spaces both indoors and outdoors, including playgrounds, gardens, an indoor gym, a creativity space, and a library with an infant-toddler corner. The shared library displays books at child's-eye level and offers comfortable seating that invites book exploration. The library was created as a community partnership with a local public library as a part of a graduate student's research project.

An indoor gym is perfect for play when the weather outside isn't welcoming. The low slides and steps are safe for toddler big body play.

In a shared creativity space, light shines through a colored-water bottle board, and a cozy nook invites children to snuggle with soft pillows.

Outside, the play space offers traditional areas such as a sandbox, sturdy swings, and a playhouse.

It also offers an intriguing garden area. Gardens don't require a huge amount of space. You just need some safe, interesting plants and a layout that invites exploration. Rocks, tree slices, and even plants can create inviting paths. The green tunnel stays about 10 degrees Fahrenheit cooler than the surrounding garden on hot days. Bird feeders, birdbaths, and flowers attract butterflies, birds, and squirrels. A couple of chairs make a cozy conversation space. Bridges offer play potential as story props or stages. Gnomes and fairies add a touch of whimsy.

A planter stores its own water, ready for a helper to water the outdoor plants. Bamboo wind chimes create soothing sounds, and a wooden pallet with metal implements attached just begs to be used for percussion explorations.

## The Three *I*'s in Classrooms

Every classroom can become more inviting, interesting, and intriguing. Whether you are rethinking an existing classroom environment or planning an entirely new one in a center, the work begins with the physical space. Picture an empty classroom as the box created by the walls, floor, and ceiling. This is a box filled with potential.

The National Association for the Education of Young Children (NAEYC) recommends a minimum of 35 square feet of useable floor space per child indoors and 75 square feet per child outdoors. Some US agencies and European countries recommend 45–50 square feet of usable indoor space per child. State child-care licensing agencies have requirements for square footage that vary by state. In my experience, providing extra space beyond the minimum required will result in calmer, more focused play and fewer visibly stressed children and teachers. A French study (Legendre, 1995) found that providing 54 square feet per child minimized conflicts, promoted positive interactions, and resulted in lower levels of the stress hormone cortisol in children. It can be challenging to find additional usable space, but that space might be as close as the hallway outside your door, as long as teachers can see and hear the children at all times.

Child-care professionals and young children spend the majority of their time in their classrooms. Intentional planning can transform these spaces into places where adults and children will look forward to spending the day.

## Inviting Classrooms

Think about the needs of all of the people who use the classroom. Provide wide pathways to allow ease of movement between play areas and to accommodate people with special needs. For example, wider doorways accommodate wheelchairs and also allow easier entrance for strollers and buggies.

Natural light through windows or skylights gives us a feeling of well-being. If you have windows, let the light in and allow the children to see the outdoor spaces. Primary colors can be overwhelming. Keep the bright colors to a minimum, leaving them mainly to those displayed in children's work. On the walls, paint in comforting, natural colors. Instead of vivid primary and secondary tones, offer enticing textures on the walls and rugs, such as smooth, padded, soft, and bumpy.

**Universal Design:** Planning for people with exceptionalities benefits everyone.

Provide functional storage to minimize clutter and allow books and materials to be changed out for different lessons and units of study. Display the materials attractively on low shelves in ways that children or adults can easily access them. Use shelving to divide the room into designated areas for play.

Provide comfortable tables and chairs for children. Children's feet should touch the floor when they are eating or working at a table. This has the added benefit of increased independence because the toddlers and twos can get up when they are finished and don't have to wait for an adult to let them out of a highchair. Provide comfortable seating for all of the adults, too: gliders for reading and rocking and low seating to support caregivers' backs when playing with children on the floor.

## Interesting Classrooms

Toys and materials look different when you get down to the floor level, compared to adult height. To understand the children's perspective, it helps to get down to their level and see what things look like.

Babies, toddlers, and twos love to try to fit their bodies onto empty shelves and other cozy spaces. They also like to see what objects will fit inside any container, from bags to purses to boxes.

Children love investigating living things. Caring for living things increases children's sense of responsibility and empathy. Some programs allow pets in the classrooms. Others keep animals in a central location or even outside in a school barnyard for all of the classes to visit. If possible, include living things, such as plants, fish, or other pets.

An interesting classroom offers lots of artistic opportunities. Toddlers are drawn to markers, fat crayons, and sidewalk chalk. Consider taping large pieces of paper to the floor, the playground fence, or covering an entire table and letting the children explore making marks. I know a teacher who sometimes tapes paper to the

underside of a table and lets two-year-olds lie on their backs and reach up to color from a new perspective. Children also love natural clay, homemade dough, nontoxic paint, bubble painting, and gadget printmaking.

The Tyson Center provides low-cost and no-cost loose parts for use in open-ended art explorations in the classroom. Some materials are donated by families in the program and businesses in the community. Young children love to investigate these textures and materials.

Of course, they provide infants and toddlers with clean items that they can safely explore and are large enough not to be choking hazards, such as the following:

| | | |
|---|---|---|
| Empty boxes | Fabric samples and scraps | Construction paper |
| New or sanitized egg cartons | Blueprints | Wrapping paper |
| Restaurant takeout containers | Magazines | Newspapers |
| Cups | Lids | Cord |
| Pine cones | Large beads | Ribbon |
| Empty tin cans (no sharp edges) | Foam shapes | Spools |
| Paper bags | Large puzzle pieces | Yarn |
| Oatmeal cans | Chenille stems | Large pompoms |
| | Tissue paper | Rulers |
| | | Cardboard tubes |

Teachers are more likely to use loose parts and to recycle/reuse art materials when the items are organized and accessible; the Tyson Center keeps the loose parts in a storeroom. It's a good idea to assign a staff member or classroom each month to

reorganize the storage space. Otherwise, just like a neglected bulletin board, it will quickly become cluttered and less useful.

Not every classroom has easy access to the outside, but it's worth the effort to play outside every day. Babies, toddlers, and twos—and their teachers—will benefit physically and emotionally from spending at least some time outdoors every day that weather permits. On days that are much too hot or cold for even a quick recess, adults and children still need a break from the classroom for a little while. Take the whole class together or divide the children into smaller groups for a stroller walk through the hallways or around the outside of the building, or take them to play in a different part of the school.

The Tyson Center offers patios off each classroom, where children can play and be outside in the fresh air. This arrangement allows for indoor/outdoor centers and provides a lovely connection to the surrounding neighborhood. Children can wave to people walking on the sidewalk below and watch cars and trucks drive past. They can observe plants and trees as the seasons change.

## Intriguing Classrooms

Good design allows a classroom to function while also providing a sense of beauty and fascination. The ceiling is like an additional wall; it's the perfect place to hang beautiful art or natural objects. If allowed by your licensing regulations, cover fluorescent lights with magnet-edged fabric covers or translucent inserts with photos of clouds, tree canopies, oceans, animals, or other nature scenes. These are especially attractive to children when they are located above cribs or changing tables; it's almost like having a light table on the ceiling. Light plays on reflective surfaces nearby.

Colors, textures, and shapes draw children's attention and entice them to explore. Interesting colors of fabric scraps and other loose parts, such as small tiles, lids, and stones, allow children to explore and imagine new uses. Organic shapes in furniture, materials, and even walkways draw us in and make us feel comfortable and relaxed. Bumpy, smooth, rough, and soft textures invite children's exploration. Focal points draw your eye, but there should also be areas of blank space where children's eyes can rest and feel calm.

At the Tyson Center, abundant natural light, raised platforms, a variety of textures, and mirrors make the classrooms inviting. Ceiling fascinations display art and beauty overhead. Both real and artificial plants feel calming and create connections between the indoor and outdoor environments.

Cozy nooks feel inviting and encourage snuggling up with a friend to look at a favorite book or just have some quiet time.

A kitchen play area and hats, ribbons, and scarves encourage pretend play. Intriguing displays, such as a wooden turntable with inviting moving parts, a texture wall, sequin mermaid fabric, prisms on a window, and loose parts in a sensory table invite children's exploration.

## Depth of Engagement: A Deeper Dive

- In your classroom, get down to the children's height and look around. What is inviting? What immediately catches your eye? What draws you in?

- Now look a little deeper. What is interesting? What makes you want to learn more?

- What is intriguing? What makes you really think? What makes you want to try out a new idea to see what happens?

- Make a list of words to describe your classroom habitat.

- What do you see? hear? feel? smell?

- What changes would you make if you could do anything to improve your classroom habitat?

# CHAPTER 3

## Age-Appropriate Environments

An age-appropriate environment provides for the needs of its inhabitants. People under three need nurturing, safe spaces where they can develop, learn, and grow. And they certainly do grow quickly! Their needs change as their skills and abilities blossom, so the environment must change along with them.

## Grouping Children into Classrooms

A central concern for many programs serving our youngest citizens is how best to form classroom groups. Classroom requirements vary according to the age of the babies in group care. NAEYC has guidelines based on children's ages for maximum group sizes and ratios for the number of children per each adult in a classroom. Relationships between caregivers, the children, and their families become stronger when they are able to stay together over longer periods of time. Attachment bonds become stronger and children feel less stress when educators minimize transitions throughout the school day and over months or years.

### Multi-Age Classrooms

In the continuity-of-care model, children of several different ages are grouped together. These groups remain together for longer periods of time, similar to the multi-age groupings in many family child-care homes. Challenges of implementing

this model, for most programs operating within a limited budget, include the higher cost per classroom. Smaller group sizes are more expensive because more staff are required to maintain adult-child ratios. For example, a classroom with four babies and five young toddlers requires three teachers.

One possible way to address both continuity and group size is through looping. *Looping* is the practice of keeping a group of children with the same teachers as the children grow older. It is another way of extending the time each child spends with the same teachers whom they already know and love. When a teacher loops, she moves from one classroom to the next with the same group of children. Groups may move from a room with cribs and highchairs to one with cots and tables for meals.

## Classrooms for Young Infants

Child-care regulations generally define nonmobile infants as babies from about six weeks old until they begin to crawl at around six to ten months old. Programs may have classrooms that serve only these babies or may offer classrooms for multiple ages. Young infants need appropriate furniture, nurturing and responsive care, and interesting items to safely explore.

For safety, nonmobile infants need the protection of shelves, low walls, room dividers, or gate systems during floor time. This prevents mobile babies and toddlers who are crawling and walking from accidentally bumping into the little ones, curiously grabbing at their faces or hair, or taking their pacifiers or toys away. Because young babies sleep according to their own schedules, gates are also useful for creating a sleeping area. The gates can separate cribs in a quieter part of the room so infants' naps are not disturbed. Of course, teachers must still be able to supervise by seeing and hearing the babies.

We used to think that the youngest infants were not very responsive and that they just needed to be fed and diapered. Now we know that babies are already learning inside the womb. Teachers and parents are the best toys for the youngest babies. By responding to their expressions and sounds, we let them know that the world is a trustworthy place. By responding to their cries and feeding them when they are hungry, promptly changing soiled diapers, and helping them go to sleep when they are tired, we are teaching them to expect that their needs will be met. Responsive caregiving builds a child's sense of trust and future capabilities.

Between the ages of two and four months, babies discover another first toy: their hands. They are mesmerized by their hands as they begin to explore the fascinating new possibilities of reaching for and grasping things. Wait to offer heavy toys, such as rattles, until young infants become fairly proficient with their hands. If offered too early, babies will drop rattles or other toys, often onto their faces. Instead, offer

safe items for nonmobile babies to explore, such as small stuffed animals, scarves, handkerchiefs, and cloth or wicker balls. Babies this age also enjoy cushy carpets and soft rugs, unbreakable mirrors, black-and-white graphics, faces, board books, soft blocks, and water-filled mats with floating toys inside. They enjoy cuddling and playing repetitive games, such as making faces and sounds back and forth with trusted adults.

## Classrooms for Mobile Infants

Once babies begin to scoot and crawl, their world opens up to new and interesting possibilities. This age is usually defined from about six to ten months to twelve to fourteen months, the age a baby typically begins to walk. Children this age have a real preference for being held upright and will bounce by bending their knees as they build muscles for walking. Mobile infants love sitting up and pulling up. They also need floor time to strengthen their arms and core muscles so they can push up and start the process of crawling. There are many ways babies move. Some roll or squirm commando-style flat across the floor. Others scoot in a sitting position, and some babies skip crawling altogether.

Babies this age are curious and will move toward anything they notice. They are attracted to, for example, lights and interesting colors in mobiles, and many love to see and touch other babies. This in an opportunity to teach them to use soft touches when reaching out to friends. Check every day for potential hazards within their reach—and this range is continually expanding. My niece used to refer to this zone as the "baby line." We had to be aware of the changing boundary where her baby could reach potentially dangerous objects. Make sure that outlets are covered when not in use, and replace the covers after using them. Cover sharp corners on furniture and cabinets. Make sure tables and chairs are sturdy enough not to tip over when mobile infants pull up on them. Provide only nontoxic art supplies, and keep cleaning supplies out of reach. Remind staff and parents to keep purses, backpacks, and diaper bags in a spot inaccessible to the babies.

## Classrooms for Toddlers

Definitions vary, but toddlerhood generally includes one-year-old and sometimes two-year-old children. It begins when babies consistently pull up and cruise around the edges of furniture and then start to take their first independent steps. Babies normally begin to walk between nine and fifteen months. This new freedom brings about lots of changes in behavior. Toddlers want so badly to practice walking that

they barely slow down long enough to eat. They need lots of safe spaces for walking and interest centers to travel between. Soon they will be running, tentatively climbing steps, and walking sideways. They are excited to try new challenges and conquer any obstacles in their paths.

## Classrooms for Twos

Two-year-olds are anything but terrible. They are some of the most entertaining people to hang around. They are adventurous and funny. And when they do get angry, they don't hold grudges. They are easily distracted from their anger or frustration by anything new that they haven't tried yet.

Engaging classrooms for two-year-old children should have a CD player or smart speaker to play and replay their favorite dance tunes and songs to sing. Arrange activities into cozy centers where they can play in small groups. Artwork and nature collections hung from the ceiling will bring the room closer to a child-size scale. Because their bodies are growing rapidly, they will continually want to test their balance and large-muscle capabilities. Climbers, steps, and slides are popular indoors and out for big-body play. Many two-year-olds love to push dolls in strollers and shopping carts. At this age, they begin to explore pretend roles with capes and costumes. They love to imitate cooking and cleaning and will use whatever props are available to mimic the work of adults that they have watched. They may use blocks as pretend make-up and use a cardboard tube as a vacuum cleaner. Their classrooms need lots of shelves for art supplies, games, loose parts, blocks, trains and cars, balls, ramps, and books. They will enjoy painting at an easel at child height and exploring sand and water in a sensory table. Their classrooms need to have individual cubbies to store coats, shoes, and bags or backpacks. At the changing table, steps are especially useful for this age and save wear on caregivers' backs. Twos also need an easily accessible toilet; expect accidents. Encourage them to develop more independence by helping dress themselves and put on their own shoes and socks.

One of the best ways to learn about innovative ideas and to find out what does and doesn't work is to visit other classrooms and talk to the teachers and directors at other centers. A wide variety of early childhood programs is available, each with its own mission, goals, and location; consequently, classrooms may be as unique as snowflakes. Even though programs may look and function differently, most early education programs do have common goals.

- All programs want the best possible experience for their staff and the families they serve.

- All programs want young children to learn and grow.

- All programs want children to be safe and happy.

Individual definitions of excellence may be unique to each site when compared to other high-quality programs with different goals and limitations. Even if there were a perfect one-size-fits-all plan, it might not meet the needs or preferences of every child and family. Each program should strive for continuous improvement: to start where they are today and become the best that they can be.

◆ ◆ ◆

Sometimes babies, toddlers, and twos like to march (or crawl or roll) to the beat of their own drum. At other times, everyone wants to do the same thing all at once. Consider everything that happens in your classroom each day—from planned lessons to surprises. Use the Daily Schedule chart and the Examining Children's

Activities and Interests chart in chapter 7 on pages 91–93 and make a list of the types of activities children and adults are doing throughout the day, such as the following:

o **Adult routines:** cleaning, preparing food, feeding, diapering or toileting, and record keeping

o **Children's independent activities:** tummy time or floor time (young infants), exploring materials (toddlers), and pretending, creating, and experimenting (two-year-olds)

o **Children's self-selected group activities:** listening to stories and poems, singing, doing fingerplays and other fine-motor play, playing with blocks, exploring loose parts, pretending, engaging in big body play, and heading outside in a stroller or buggy or going on walks

   1. Consider arranging the room to better accommodate these activities.

   2. Create a daily schedule of when the adults and children typically engage in these activities and tasks.

   3. Examine the daily routine to notice how often group and independent activities occur. Consider changes to the day that would minimize transitions and allow the children to make more choices.

# CHAPTER 4

**Language Development:
Environments to Talk About**

The language arts include listening, speaking, reading, writing, viewing, and visually representing. Young children develop these skills in a literacy-rich environment filled with the busy hum of talking, singing, and music, as well as quiet time to reflect. They need opportunities to hear stories, hold picture books, make marks, and look at photographs and artwork. Childhood is a sensitive period of development. Sensitive periods are times when the brain is primed for learning. For example, humans learn a second language best from about age five until about the age of seventeen. After that, we can still learn a new language, but we won't be able to pronounce the sounds like a native speaker (Hartshorne, Tenenbaum, and Pinker, 2018).

## Cozy Corners and Book Nooks

"Over in the meadow in the sand in the sun lived an old mother turtle and her little turtle one." This is the beginning line of one of my favorite childhood stories. According to family lore, I would follow my brothers around the house with the *Over in the Meadow* (Wadsworth, 1962) picture book, begging them to read it over and over until I had all the words memorized. I loved that book, with its old-fashioned watercolor illustrations. I loved the melodic pattern of the words and the number patterns building up to ten. I loved the nurturing lessons as each of the animal mothers teaches her baby a new life skill. These days I can appreciate the crisp, bright, newer editions of this rhyming story, but the old hardcovers, with their finely detailed pictures and picture-book smell, transport me back to my childhood like a time machine. Why does this happen? Because books are more than print, and story time is more than words—it is a memory in the making.

Literacy centers in our classrooms invite young children to interact with books. Infant, toddler, and twos classrooms should each have their own story corner classroom library. Classroom libraries matter because they provide a cozy space to cuddle up and share a book with a child or two. Sometimes the whole group will squeeze in together to look at books. Impromptu big-group story time often pops up with toddlers, who tend to travel together in a pack to wherever the action is in the room. In a literacy corner, you'll want to have lots of books; you might aim for five to seven books per child. Remember, classroom libraries can also include books borrowed temporarily from the center supply room or public library. You'll want nonfiction books as well as fiction, books with photographs as well as drawings, and well-written stories that adults and children will enjoy hearing over and over again.

Books for people under three need to be durable. Look for books with vinyl covers, board books, plastic books, or cloth books. As a bonus, these books are easier to sanitize between uses. Because young children explore books and toys with their mouths, we want babies to have "books to chew on." They learn about the world through all of their senses, including taste and touch. They get lots of information about taste and texture by mouthing books and toys, so they need to have books that will not be ruined by this natural exploration. Luckily, more and more picture books are printed in durable formats.

The literacy corner doesn't have to be located in a corner of the classroom. Books should be accessible anywhere in the room that makes sense to have them. A large basket of books next to a glider near the cribs will be useful for helping a child settle down to take a nap. This would be a perfect place to have a collection of peaceful, calming books to read softly as a child drifts off to sleep. A dress-up center with clothes and props for dramatic play is a good place to include picture books that feature children from around the world dressed in ordinary, everyday clothes and dressed up for special cultural events. Classroom libraries should reflect the diversity that exists in the classroom and in the world. Books, toys, and posters should include a range of ages, sizes, skin tones, hair textures, gender roles, and abilities. Books about different types of restaurants could be paired with costumes specific to those professions. A chef's hat and apron and a box of felt scraps create props for making pretend pizzas. Pair these props with books such as *Pete's a Pizza* by William Steig or *Pete the Cat and the Perfect Pizza Party* by Kimberly and James Dean. A waiter's apron and menus, combined with dishes and a table, pair with picture books, such as *Dim Sum for Everyone* by Grace Lin or *Froggy Eats Out* by Jonathan London, in a restaurant play center. A gross motor center could feature books that encourage big body movement, such as *Yoga Pretzels* by Tara Gruber. Photos of yoga poses and a yoga mat will inspire children to try them out. Some sparkly dance costumes can be paired with books featuring human dancers or the animals in Sandra Boynton's *Barnyard Dance*. Children's theaters, dance studios, or parents with older children might be willing to donate old costumes.

Transitions can be challenging. Consider placing some of the class's favorite read-aloud books near the doorway where parents drop children off and where children wait for parents to pick them up. The books could help children ease into their school day and make the transition away from their parents in the morning and could serve as a distraction for those waiting at the end of the day.

Consider adding a child-sized sofa or chair to your library area or creating a cozy little space with cushions. A lower cabinet with the door taken off or a cardboard box can become a favorite cozy place for looking at books alone or with a friend. For sensory interest, attach some inviting textures onto the sides of the box, such as a fuzzy rug or some smooth, shiny fabric on one side and coarse woven fabric on another side. Leave one side and the top open for better visibility. A fabric tablecloth and some dried or silk flowers, a small rug, and beautiful cushions make a reading corner more inviting. Display favorite books with an air of celebration, and introduce new books with fanfare.

## The Strength of Stories

I've heard teachers say, "Now we're really learning," when they get to a lesson about letters and numbers, but everything we do in the classroom—both planned and unplanned—is actually teaching. The children are learning from everything that happens around them. Lessons on friendship and kindness are every bit as important as lessons about numbers and letter sounds. Children do not need to be seated or looking at a screen to be learning. They are learning all of the time from everything they see, hear, and do.

Children can learn more deeply and apply their ideas to new situations better when they actively participate in the learning process. Participation includes singing, listening, speaking, doing, and even watching others. These experiences are especially meaningful in the context of everyday life activities. Playing with real objects helps children build the background understanding they will use later when they begin to read and write. Telling stories about what has happened during the day helps children remember the things that happened, put them in order, and develop oral-language fluency. Narrating a child's actions like a sportscaster helps them think about what they are doing at the present moment—"Raven, you have a block in your hand. You carried it to the kitchen area. Where will you put it? You put the block inside the play oven. Are you baking?" Children also need opportunities to tell their own stories, even before we understand what they are saying. We need to pause and give them time to speak. Sometimes they will show us what they are talking about, and sometimes we will have to respectfully imagine what it is that they intended to say.

We can help families see the future academic value in the things they are already doing by encouraging them to have conversations with their children each day. We can include information about our classroom activities in daily reports, on classroom websites, or in newsletters: "Ask me about what the children have been exploring in the sensory center." When we include photos, parents understand what their child is doing all day in our program, and we can offer ideas for families to expand literacy skills through informal storytelling at home. Many families do this already, but they may need to be reminded how valuable it is to listen, sing, and speak with their children every day. These opportunities help their children develop language fluency right now and will continue to promote their future success in school.

## The World On and Beyond the Walls

Picture the walls in your classroom. Walls are important because they create the atmosphere of the room and give the children something to talk about. Children appreciate beautiful art prints and nature mobiles as much as adults do. Fabric draped from the ceiling (if licensing allows) brings the room closer to a child-sized scale. Fabrics and wall carpet help absorb sound. Many classrooms put up educational bulletin boards. However, children don't pay much attention to teacher-store cut-outs like shapes and colors. Shapes and colors are fine to include in conversations when they relate to work the child is doing, but stapled up, they are just wallpaper. Children will learn more from photos of their own families and

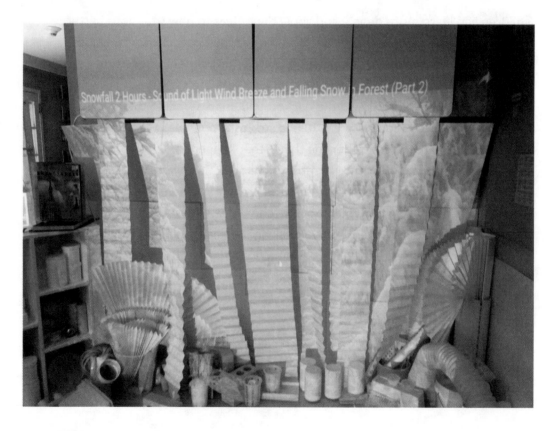

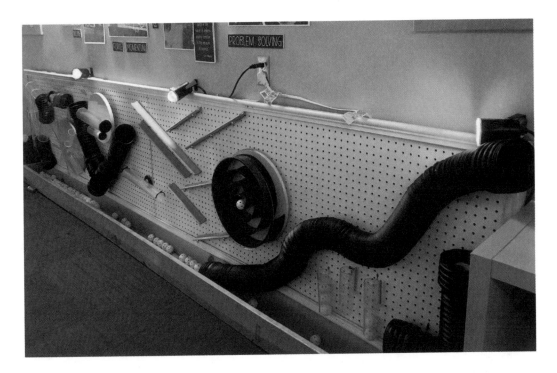

classmates, displayed at a level that they can view, which will spark meaningful conversations.

Talk about a wide variety of topics in the context of daily classroom life. Teacher-store posters and word walls are not necessary for babies and toddlers. Displays of print without a clear purpose just become visual clutter. I've found that children respond best to displays of work they've created themselves. They respond more to things created by their teachers than they respond to preprinted teaching posters on the wall. When children's work is respectfully displayed, it makes the entire classroom more beautiful.

If your space has windows, uncover them as often as possible so that children can see what's going on outside. If your windows are too high for the children to see out, think about building carpet-covered steps or stages so the children can climb up to see outside better. When children can see the outdoors, they can talk about what they see and think about what they want to do later on a walk around the building or on the playground, depending on the view. Sometimes there is excitement on the street outside, such as a squirrel running with an acorn in its mouth or a trash truck lumbering by. These events provide opportunities to introduce new vocabulary words. The weather outside and changing seasons with budding flowers and falling leaves will give you plenty to talk about with children.

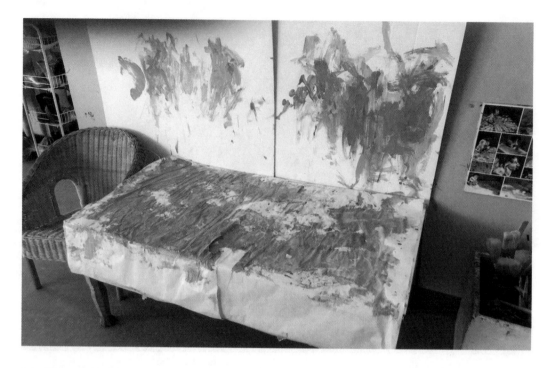

## Making Marks

To develop writing skills, children just need a surface to write on and some art tools for making marks. Large sheets of paper, concrete sidewalks, whiteboards, chalkboards, easels, and tabletops can all be good surfaces for writing with washable markers or chalk. Toddlers will grasp and squeeze tight with their whole hands, so they need large, sturdy tools such as big crayons, sidewalk chalk, or even washable nontoxic Bingo daubers. Sidewalk chalk can be used indoors or out, on paper or cement. If you cover an entire table with paper, you won't have to worry about where the marks go as children learn to control the markers and develop eye-hand coordination. Toddlers love washable, nontoxic magic markers. Some teachers find that unscented markers are less likely to be taste-tested by the children. Adults will need to help children retrieve markers that roll away and make sure the lids snap down tight to prevent the markers from drying out when they are not in use. Two-year-olds enjoy experimenting with both fine- and thick-tipped markers and with crayons of various shapes, including multi-colored "cupcakes." Create these recycled crayons by melting broken bits of old crayons together in a cupcake tin placed in an oven at a low temperature. Allow the crayon cupcakes to solidify into disc shapes as they cool.

The children will also enjoy trying different papers, such as grocery bags, newsprint, manila paper, construction paper, and even wrapping paper, to see how the different art tools work on each surface. Pens and pencils are especially appealing because of their associations with adults' work. Creating hand-made marks on paper with children gives us an opportunity to slow down from the busyness of our teaching day and appreciate children's creativity while we talk to them about the process of making their artwork.

Children all over the world scribble in very similar, predictable ways before they begin to draw or write, according to psychologist and early childhood educator Rhoda Kellogg (Walsh, 2020). Adults can describe a child's scribbling and try to imitate it, but we are no longer truly capable of scribbling freely and expressively as a child because we overthink it. Artist Pablo Picasso (1881–1973) is reported to have said that he spent his lifetime relearning to draw like a child. Once we are past our own childhoods, we no longer really understand the world as a child experiences it. We can only understand as outsiders looking back. Young preschoolers often draw a head and face on a circle with arms and legs sticking out from the sides. This "bug body" is kind of how our own bodies appear to us as we look at our bodies from inside them. It might be how we appear to ourselves before we understand that mirrors reflect the way that other people see our bodies. Children's scribbles and drawings help us understand how the world looks through their eyes. Children's early figure drawing might start with a dog. Then rounded ears become pointy and voilà! It's a cat. Longer legs transform this basic drawing into a horse or cow. Rotate the body to stand upright and it becomes a person. In the 2011 film *Eric Carle, Picture Writer: The Art of the Picture Book*, children's-book author and illustrator Eric Carle believed that children deserve big sheets of paper, bright paint, and large paintbrushes to express their ideas with their big body movements. He said his own books, such as *The Very Hungry Caterpillar*, are intentionally nurturing to help children make the transition from home to school.

# CHAPTER 5

## Cognitive Development:
## Environments to Think About

At first glance, it may seem that science, technology, engineering, and math (STEM) activities are beyond what people under three are capable of. But if you think about it, these activities are perfect for young children because they are designed to help children do what they do naturally:

- Find out more about the natural world
- Use tools for practical purposes
- Solve problems
- Explore number

All of the STEM disciplines build upon young children's inborn desire to know more. Lessons in STEM can be especially effective for children with special needs. Discovery learning promotes a sense of joy and self-confidence. Teachers can adapt lessons so that each child can feel successful.

The worlds inhabited by people under three years old are a lot like those of older children and adults. They are also special and unique for several reasons. People who are not yet communicating clearly, and those not yet speaking at all, rely on the rest of us to interpret their needs and wishes. As they develop, children's brains are shaped by their daily experiences and interactions. Enriched environments enhance growth, but abuse, neglect, and impoverished environments diminish it. As early childhood professionals, it is our duty to protect and nurture our youngest citizens and to provide respectful environments that promote their health, growth, happiness, curiosity, love, and understanding.

## Open Ended, Not Overwhelming

How can we encourage young children's thinking and engage their minds? Thoughtfully selected materials and intentionally planned lessons can support children's own ideas and scaffold to new learning. Infant-toddler and twos classrooms can be visually overstimulating, with primary-colored walls and rugs and with shelves filled with bright plastic toys spilling and scattered across the floor. I have visited rooms filled with an assortment of containers to buckle babies into or otherwise limit their motion: swings, bouncy seats, foam chairs, highchairs, cribs, car seats, and strollers. Many of these containers come with their own toys attached. Some states' regulations do not allow babies to be placed in bouncy seats

or swings; others limit their use to 20 minutes at a time. Containers limit babies' movement and muscle development. People under three need to be able to wiggle, roll, grasp, crawl, pull up, and walk as they discover what their bodies can do and investigate interesting things in the environment.

Toys can teach thinking skills. We may think of educational toys as those with letters and numbers, but these toys may not encourage children to develop new thoughts and ideas. What if some or all of the usual toys were replaced with more interesting and engaging materials? An infant-toddler or twos classroom without any toys sounds like an evil plot cooked up by an old TV-show villain. Why would anyone want to deprive children of toys? Toys are fun. They should help children learn and feel happy. But are there some toys that are better for young children than others? Let's reconsider what we think of as toys. In some schools, loose-parts play has replaced more traditional toys in their classrooms.

Toys have changed over the last few generations. Children have always played with anything they could reach and explore. My mother was given scraps of dough to play with as her mother made biscuits. Modern toys have evolved from whatever children could find to very specific representations. An action figure comes with its own backstory and scripts for children to play out. As a proud member of Generation X, my own childhood memories include baby dolls and Barbies, teddy bears, and Hot Wheels. These toys were more specific than those of my parents' generation, but my toys' adventures were limited only by my imagination. My own children showed an early interest in electronic games. Minecraft was one of their more open-ended interests. When building with actual blocks, they tried to recreate the virtual worlds they had built in Minecraft. They tried to follow the Lego and K'nex instruction booklets to build exact replicas of the picture on the box. Children today have highly specific models that have been scaled down from the adult world. Intricate details define the toys to specific uses and limit their play possibilities. Although children love to dress as favorite characters and reenact movie scenes, very specific movie- or cartoon-themed toys and costumes do not encourage children to use their imaginations to create new plots and stories. When my child continued to wear a flower-girl dress long past the wedding, people would stop and ask her, "Which princess are you?" implying that all princesses come from Disney.

Think about two toy figurines: a comic-book hero and a wooden peg person. The first one has its own name, a voice you might already be hearing in your head, and an expected role to play. The second one could be a man, a woman, a grandparent, a baby, or a child. It could be a chef, traffic cop, brick mason, company president, or superhero. The play potential is far less limited because its story hasn't been predefined.

Consider two toy trucks: one a plastic firetruck and the other a nonspecific wooden block vehicle.

The first one has a particular job to do and sounds to make. The second one could become a family van, a dump truck, a school bus, a golf cart, an ice cream truck, or even a firetruck. It's up to the children playing to decide their own adventure.

We need to select toys for their play potential. My dad used say, "Things are made to sell," meaning that we shouldn't really be disappointed when they break because the focus was on moving merchandise, not long-term durability. To sell, toys need to grab a consumer's attention and convince someone to make the purchase. Some toys are created to sound very loud so they'll be heard by shoppers in noisy big-box stores or light up or sparkle to look exciting as shoppers scroll through online ads. As teachers, we need to think beyond the point of sale to the long-term goals of our classroom. Passive toys make active children.

How we set up a classroom reflects what we believe about children and learning. Montessori materials, for example, are designed to focus a child's attention on a single variable at a time, such as weight, height, or color. Dr. Maria Montessori (1870–1952) believed that, when given a choice, children choose work that challenges their current level of understanding. The teacher's role is to plan the environment and support the children's growing independence. Children are drawn toward activities that allow them to practice concepts over and over until they understand them fully. By isolating each attribute, Montessori materials help children organize their thinking by creating their own understanding of concepts.

Today's educational toys include variety in sizes, shapes, colors, and sounds, often within the same toy. For example, in Montessori's iconic material, the pink tower, the ten wooden blocks are all the same color, texture, and shape. The only change from one block to the next is in size. This allows children to think about the graduated difference of each block as they carry it from the shelf to the work mat. In contrast, in the classic stacking rings toy, each plastic "donut" differs in color as well as size, and some versions also light up and make electronic sounds. The intent is probably to teach multiple skills more efficiently, but the result may be confusion and sensory overload. I have observed children trying the different rings randomly, without thinking about which one ought to come next in the sequence.

## The Sounds of Science

Early childhood teachers seek that just-right "Goldilocks" space, where lessons aren't so hard that they are frustrating for a child and not so easy that they become boring. Psychologist Lev Vygotsky (1896–1934) described this just-right space where a child is intellectually available for learning as the zone of proximal development (ZPD). The young child is like a scientist: always learning, always seeking to know more than they currently do. The ZPD can be described as the space between what is known and what is next. For infants and toddlers, this means providing materials that capture their attention and invite further exploration. To meet children where they are today and help them move toward the next step of understanding, we need to become careful observers of the children in our class.

If we watch closely, children will show us what they need at any moment. Responsive teachers present the children with interesting materials that appeal to their senses. As children show interest, we can extend their thinking by adding new parts or creating unexpected events to capture their attention. By watching their responses, we get an idea of where we should take the lesson next. For example, if a baby accidentally kicks over a small popcorn tin behind her while lying on her tummy, she may be startled by the noise and seek reassurance from an adult nearby. If the adult narrates the event like a sportscaster, "You kicked that over. It was a little loud. Do you want to try again?" and then replaces the can by the baby's foot, the stage is set for the child to try to recreate the response with the same movements. The movements may be accidental at first but will become more intentional with each repetition, rewarded by the satisfying crashing sound and the adult's response. Discovery, investigation, creativity, and problem-solving opportunities are vital aspects of playful learning.

## Loose Parts of Engaging Play

Have you seen children push a toy aside for the box it came in? Have you noticed children fascinated by the tools in a toolbox or pans in the cabinets? Where does this fascination come from? Children like to mimic the adults they watch and imitate their work. Another reason is the greater potential for play in these materials. Cardboard containers can be used in many ways. Hands, arms, and sometimes whole bodies can fit inside. The flaps can be opened and closed. Cardboard has a papery texture that holds up well to being decorated with markers, tape, and scraps of paper. Lots of toys are less interesting to explore because they don't appeal to all five senses. Natural materials, such as loofah sponges and leaves,

or even ordinary household tools such as kitchen gadgets provide greater learning potential than some toys, even those that are labeled as educational.

Inspired by the early childhood programs in Reggio Emilia, Italy, some child-care programs across the United States and around the world are reconsidering what they think of as playthings. Classrooms are incorporating more real objects and recycled materials for children to investigate. These teachers take a supportive role, asking questions, writing down ideas, and taking photographs to revisit with the children later, as they plan their next steps in learning. Rethinking classroom toys isn't about throwing everything out. It's about becoming a careful observer, a detective, watching each child intently to see what he is telling us with his actions. Children's behaviors reveal information that their words might not be able to tell us.

Teachers who observe what children find interesting can help extend their thinking by adding similar, more challenging objects. This doesn't mean changing everything out each day. Give each item some time, maybe a couple of weeks, even when everyone ignores it at first. Reintroduce things again after a few weeks before you give up on them. Each child will have different preferences that will change as the child develops more skills. Each group will have favorite things that will change from year to year.

Open-ended materials promote creativity and multiple ways of understanding. Setting up your classroom for discovery learning will create a calmer, more intentional space with children eager to explore the properties of the materials. As the children focus on figuring out all about the interesting, sensory-rich objects around them, there will be less fussing from boredom and less crying in general because attention is focused positively on exploration. The busy hum of activity allows teachers to accomplish caregiving routines more effectively, to enjoy their time in the classroom, and to experience lower stress levels.

## Low- and No-Cost Heuristic Materials

The term *heuristic* comes from the Greek word *heuriskein*, which is also where the word *eureka* ("I have found it!") comes from. *Heuriskein* means "discovery." Exploring the treasures in a basket of natural and household items, children seem to be considering the play potential of each object they pick up. Even babies who might just bang the pieces together and drop them on the floor or back into the basket seem to be evaluating the materials. We would typically expect an attention span of about 40 seconds for a four-month-old child, but I have observed babies spend up to 45 minutes exploring ordinary household objects.

Babies want to explore the interesting taste, textures, and smells and compare the weights and surface temperatures of different items. They might show surprise at the squishiness of a sponge or the stiffness of the bristles on a brush. Babies love stainless steel measuring cups and spoons. The shiny, cool surfaces are inviting to touch and taste, and they reflect light in interesting ways. Older toddlers may use

drumsticks like giant chopsticks, using them to lift and move leaves from one spot to another. Two-year-olds might stack old CDs back into the center post of their holder while marveling at the shiny rainbow on the reflective surface. They might hang bracelets and napkin rings on a mug tree or pretend to cook dinner by stirring beads with a wooden spoon in a small silver cooking pot. Silicone kitchen gadgets such as hot pads and collapsible colanders come in bright colors and are easy to sanitize and store.

Collecting materials for this type of play in your classroom doesn't have to be expensive. If you make a list of things you'd like to have, parents can help you start your collections. Make sure all items are sanitized, unbroken with no cracks, and larger than a choke tester tube. Choosing unfinished wooden objects eliminates the risk of toxic finishes.

- **Heuristic materials for babies**
  - Cookie tins
  - Embroidered handkerchiefs
  - Loofahs and sponges
  - Coasters
  - Measuring cups

- **Heuristic materials for toddlers**
  - Containers with lids
  - Purses, bags, and beautiful things to put things inside them
  - Nesting cups or bowls
  - Measuring cups
  - Wooden spoons
  - Small pots and pans

- **Heuristic materials for twos**
  - Pretty dishes
  - Muffin tins

- Old remote controls (with the batteries removed and the little screws glued in place)

- Pine cones

- Makeup brushes

- Real fruits

- Large nuts and bolts

- Small tiles

- Ribbons to weave on a chain-link fence

- Palm-sized river rocks

## Lessons with Light

Lighting is a very important and often overlooked element of the environment. Natural light is the number one office perk for overall happiness and productivity. Light can make a space feel more inviting, and the lack of light can make it feel foreboding. Too much lighting can be overstimulating. Flickering bulbs and lighting that's too dim can cause headaches. The best light is the natural light from windows and skylights, if you're lucky enough to have windows in your classroom. Daylight can destroy mold and bacteria and provide vitamin D. If your classroom doesn't have access to natural light, you can add light through the careful placement of lamps and strings of fairy lights around the room.

Lights can also be an interactive element for the children. Add light tables, light cubes, rope lights, and ultraviolet black light centers to make translucent neon

### Make a Light Box

You'll need a clear plastic storage tote and a shop light. Cut a hole in the tote on one side at the base. Make the hole just big enough to pull the plug through. Place the light inside the box, pull the plug and cord through the hole, replace the lid firmly, and plug the light into an outlet. Position the light box against a wall, so the children cannot access the plug or cord. Supervise children closely when they are in this area.

containers glow. Mirrors, CDs, crystals, and disco balls can be used to bounce light around the room and create lovely focal points. I know of a center that added windows into solid exterior doors to let more light into the building. Children who can see trees and other plants outside their classroom windows perform better in school. But in the absence of windows, even pictures of nature have a positive effect.

Each time I've visited the Loris Malaguzzi Center in Reggio Emilia, Italy, I've been impressed with the variety of beautiful invitations to explore light and shadow. The photos and descriptions on display document young children's innovative thinking about light and space. Visitors too can explore materials that will react in unexpected ways to provoke reflection and new ideas.

You may worry that creating spaces where people under three can explore light would be expensive, but you can create light play on a budget. There are many places where you can find materials, such as the following:

- Find light strings at after-Christmas clearance sales.
- Ask public schools if they have unused overhead projectors in storage.
- Scout garage sales for slide or film projectors.
- Ask families to donate flashlights and batteries.

Provide children's books to encourage light and shadow play. You can share these with the children and then let them explore them on their own.

Boyd, Lizi. 2014. *Flashlight*. San Francisco, CA: Chronicle Books.

Brown, Margaret Wise. 1947/1975. *Goodnight Moon*. New York: Harper and Row.

Carle, Eric. 2015. *Firefly, Light Up the Sky*. Chicago, IL: PI Kids.

Kirk, Daniel. 2010. *Honk Honk! Beep Beep!* New York: Disney Hyperion.

Lionni, Leo. 1993. *Let's Make Rabbits*. Decorah, IA: Dragonfly Books.

Paulding, Barbara. 2010. *Nighttime Nursery Rhymes: A Bedtime Shadow Book*. White Plains, NY: Peter Pauper Press.

Stevenson, Robert Louis. 2011. *My Shadow*. Seattle, WA: Jackson Fish Market.

# CHAPTER 6

## Emotional Development: Nurturing Environments

Unconditional love and respect that are consistent over time will build a sense of trust with young children and their families. Every child and every family should feel as if they are secretly everyone's favorite. We build resilience by helping families see the unique gifts, inherent value, and tremendous potential of their children. We can help young children see themselves as capable and independent. When we support the toddler anthem, "I can do it myself," this resilient attitude may become the little voice inside their heads years down the road as they face the challenges of life. The people who touch our lives when we are babies have a lasting impact throughout our lifetimes.

In Montessori education, lessons of grace and courtesy directly teach children how to be kind to one another, use polite manners, and take care of classroom materials independently. Teachers model respectful treatment of others and allow opportunities for children to experience how it feels to treat others with kindness and to expect kindness in return. Maria Montessori said, "Of all things love is the most potent."

Behavior problems often occur when the environment is not responsive to children's individual needs. This means being receptive to changing moods throughout the day and adjusting our expectations as children's capabilities grow throughout the year. I visited a toddler class where the children were very fussy, the teachers were stressed to the point of quitting, and the materials were scattered all over the shelves and floor. Thinking back after the visit, I realized most of the available materials were boxes of matching games designed for elementary-age children. Of course the toddlers weren't interested in them! At that same school, the children had little to do on the playground, but I noticed a line of tricycles that were locked to the fence with a chain through the front wheels. When I asked, teachers reported that the key had been lost. They weren't sure if it was three or four years ago. They realized it might be time to get some bolt cutters or watch a YouTube video on how to open the lock.

Our classrooms can become safe havens of emotional safety in a hectic world. We can create calming, peaceful environments by adding beautiful elements such as plants and prints and by making small changes in response to the children's needs. Consideration for design, beauty, function, and the child's perspective will ensure that your classroom is a place where children and adults will enjoy spending their days. Inspiration can come from anywhere as you compile your own wonderful ideas to create nurturing, respectful places and inviting spaces for infants and toddlers.

## Baby Steps to Healthy Minds and Bodies

We need to be vigilant every day to ensure that our programs provide both physical and psychological safety. Physical safety includes following regulations for fire safety, preventing choking hazards and playground injuries, and securing classroom furniture from tipping over. Contingency planning is imagining everything that could go wrong and planning ways to keep those things from happening. Psychological safety involves feelings of emotional security, predictability, and love. Feeding involves much more than nutrients. It is a time for social bonding and reaffirming friendships and belonging.

### Psychological Safety: Loved and Nurtured

More than any other time in our lives, babyhood is all about becoming. Young children are always on the threshold of a new ability. Long before they achieve each milestone, they are practicing all the pieces of that new skill. A two-month-old can't have a conversation with a teacher—or can she? I just had a conversation with an eight-week-old. I said, "Hello," while nodding my head and making eye contact. Jemy responded with clear recognition of my voice, kicking both feet, pumping her arms, and raising both eyebrows with delight when I spoke again as she lay on a soft rug. Just a few days after meeting me, she is anything but passive about this

greeting; she is a full participant in this social exchange. She recognizes my voice and may be starting to figure out that an adult talking to her in the classroom might be followed by another event. Someone might pick her up or place something interesting beside her to look at, or perhaps the person will join her on the floor. Each of her senses is engaged. The feel of the rug or a human snuggle, the smell of shampoo or fabric softener on clothes when a person approaches, the sight of a mirror or bright toy, the taste of a pacifier or bottle—all of these stimuli give babies information to process. Jemy is learning through all of the senses at the same time. Her brain is organizing them and learning how to anticipate what might happen next. The order and combination of these events will start to form patterns that she can use to predict what's about to happen. If I often say, "Let's check that diaper," just before I lift her to the changing table, she will start to learn what's about to happen and won't be as upset by the activity because she is able to anticipate it. If I talk to her in a playful voice and explain each step of the process, she'll grow more secure in the routine. These expectations are a pathway into the next steps of physical and social development.

Young children's actions provide a window to their next achievement. Today, fifteen-month-old Josh announced that his shoe was coming loose by walking toward me across the uneven grass of the playground, his forehead wrinkled as he looked down at his shoe and then at me. His gaze said, "Fix it," even though his only word was, "Gaah." The combination of intense emotion, speech, and movement gave me the clues I needed to solve this little mystery. I can recognize the parts of this interaction that he organized like a conversation without words. Looking through this window into his development, I can see that recognizable words will be coming very soon.

When a young child is in an unfamiliar place, we need to remember that she can become stressed by the new people, smells, sounds, and sights. Calming activities can include singing a familiar song, reading a favorite story, stepping outside for a breath of fresh air, bouncing, swinging, or scooping and pouring water, sand, or other material. All children benefit from sensory experiences, but these are especially helpful for those who have sensory-processing issues to help them self-regulate. It's impossible to overstate the importance of relationships with nurturing, responsive adults for children's feelings of safety.

Young children find joy in creative expression with paint, markers, chalk, and natural clay. Even babies appreciate flowers, whether real or artificial, and beautiful arrangements of materials in the classroom. Opportunities to explore freely and become actively engaged in creative activities develop a positive sense of self and contribute to an overall sense of well-being.

# Toddler Books that Explore Feelings

Abrams Appleseed. 2017. *Making Faces: A First Book of Emotions*. New York: Abrams Appleseed.

Barnes, J. A. 2016. *Show Me How You Feel*. Cambridge, MA: Star Bright Books.

Beaumont, Karen. 2016. *I Like Myself!* New York: HMH Books for Young Readers.

Boynton, Sandra. 2011. *Happy Hippo, Angry Duck*. New York: Little Simon.

Boynton, Sandra. 2003. *Snuggle Puppy! A Little Love Song*. New York: Workman.

Carle, Eric. 1997. *The Very Quiet Cricket*. New York: Philomel Books.

Fox, Mem. 2006. *Whoever You Are*. New York: HMH Books for Young Readers.

Intrater, Roberta Grobel. 1997. *Smile!* New York: Cartwheel Books.

Johnson, Crockett. 1955/2015. *Harold and the Purple Crayon*. New York: HarperCollins.

McGrath, Layla. 2020. *Baby's Feelings: A First Book of Emotions*. Melville, NY: Little Hippo Books.

Miller, Margaret. 1998. *Baby Faces*. New York: Little Simon.

Shepherd, Jodie. 2014. *How Do You Feel?* New York: Scholastic.

Willems, Mo. 2005. *The Pigeon Has Feelings, Too!* New York: Hyperion Books for Children.

## Physical Safety: Gentle Guidance

. . . . . . . . . . . . . . . . . . . . . . . . . . . . . . . . . . . . . . . . . . . . . . . . . . . . . . . . . . . .

We've come to depend on a global positioning system (GPS) of satellites to let us know where we need to go. In a similar way, appropriate environments—environmental guidance systems (EGS), if you will—help guide young children to appropriate safe behaviors.

Early childhood teachers sometimes feel as if everybody wants to tell us what to do and how we ought to be doing our jobs. There is plenty of conventional wisdom about how we should guide and direct children's behavior. Infants elicit strong feelings, and people may not want their own ideas on child care and child guidance to be challenged. Those who staunchly defend their own traditional views can be thought of as "gatekeepers." These guardians of the status quo may be parents, grandparents, coworkers, or administrators.

However, nobody knows the people in your classroom like you do. You are the expert on the children and your space. You spend more time with these folks in this group than anyone else except your coteacher. The people who write the curriculum don't know these children like you do. Your boss probably doesn't spend as much time in this classroom as you do. Trust yourself. Trust your gut feelings. Advocate for the people in your classroom who cannot yet speak for themselves.

For example, the person telling us to move a shelf may not understand that positioning the shelf closer to the art center makes the paper and crayons easier to reach. When we're told we should move a rug, the gatekeeper might not understand that centering the rug will also cause it to block the door from opening. When we're told that a child is spending too much time in the block area and not enough in other areas, the gatekeeper might not realize that the child is focused on understanding balance. A child who doesn't seem to be paying attention may be able to recite the story you just read word for word, despite hearing it from under the table, across the room.

Change takes time. Patience and presenting evidence calmly will yield better results than belittling the gatekeepers' ideas or dismissing them altogether.

We have decades of research on techniques that will be most effective and why they work. *Guru* is ancient Sanskrit for "teacher of teachers." We are fortunate to have scores of excellent gurus in our field to look to for guidance. Two of the most influential educators and researchers are Magda Gerber and T. Berry Brazelton.

Magda Gerber was an early childhood educator and the developer of the Resources for Infant Educarers (RIE) approach. She introduced the view of infants as complete individuals with their own preferences and ideas. This view was considered controversial when it was introduced in the mid-twentieth century, but now it is backed up by current brain research. For more information on the RIE approach, see https://www.rie.org.

Pediatrician T. Berry Brazelton developed the Neonatal Behavioral Assessment Scale (NBAS) to help parents see the learning capabilities and reflexes already present in newborns. His book and video series, *Touchpoints*, have helped parents and teachers see children's developmental milestones as opportunities for guidance and learning.

The work of both Gerber and Brazelton helped us to recognize that all behavior is communication. Babies, toddlers, and two-year-olds are telling us what they need with their actions. When those actions involve hitting, biting, or other unwanted behaviors, redirection is an effective form of guidance for people under three.

When we pay careful attention, we can respond appropriately to children's cues. Far too often, adults miss these cues, and this miscommunication leads to frustration. Babies will cry when we continue to seek playful interactions after they have told us that they need a break by turning their heads away or yawning. Two-year-olds may have tantrums out of frustration for not getting something they want, but tantrums can also result from the overwhelming feeling of being misunderstood.

Young children will reflect our moods, as well. Mirror neurons cause them to imitate others' facial expressions, gaze, breathing, and even eyebrow movements. You can probably remember a time that children have responded in a completely surprising way when you thought they weren't paying any attention.

Classroom environments reflect a program's philosophy. The environment plays multiple roles in supporting physical, cognitive, and individual development. Messages from the environment should make young children and their families feel seen and heard. There are lots of curriculum options available to programs today, including the following:

- Forest schools where the majority of the learning happens outdoors
- Nature preschools that focus on outdoor walks and natural classroom materials
- Programs based on the philosophies of preschools in Reggio Emilia, Italy
- Montessori schools
- Head Start and Early Head Start
- Family home child care
- Traditional child-care programs

It's exciting to live in a time when we—teachers and parents—can choose from among a variety of schools with different child-centered approaches and environments.

## Light, Sounds, and Shapes

Lamps, light strings, and dimmer switches allow us to adjust the levels of lighting to suit the activities happening in the room. Uplighting and turning blinds to shine sunlight toward the ceiling spreads the light more naturally around the room, making the occupants feel calmer.

Sounds of nature played at quiet times of the day can reduce stress levels. Music can encourage active play and singing along at appropriate times, and there should be some quieter times with no background sounds being played at all during each day.

Curved and organic shapes in our environment make us feel more comfortable than geometric shapes with corners and straight lines, but classrooms are often filled with rectangles: ceiling tiles, cinderblock walls, tables, whiteboards, windows, floor tiles, and rugs. Think of ways you can incorporate more organic shapes and curved edges into your classroom and on your playground for a more peaceful atmosphere.

## Opportunities for Human Interaction and Active Play

During the recent global pandemic, we witnessed an unprecedented number of changes throughout the world. Some were potentially positive, such as parents who were now working from home. Families were encouraged to stay home during vacations and free time, so they were able to spend more time with their children. Society began to express more respect and appreciation for schoolteachers and child-care providers. The emphasis on handwashing, cleaning, sanitizing, and disinfecting, as well as getting more fresh air, has led to healthier practices that have resulted in fewer minor illnesses for most people. We can use the skills that we learned when we were thrown into the virtual world to continue positive outcomes, such as the convenience of virtual home visits and parent meetings that encourage more participation.

There were many negative impacts as well. Many child-care businesses were forced to close, and families struggled to make ends meet. Online classes and the need to keep children occupied greatly increased the amount of screen time for young children. Now we face the task of changing children's new habits and limiting screen time again.

Screen time interferes with what children really need: human interaction and active play. Screen time causes children to become bored too easily with real life. Games and children's programming flash images much faster than real experiences unfold. Because children's brains are still developing, they come to expect many thoughts per second, combined with sounds and light. In addition, children who are focused on screens miss opportunities to develop friendships and understand social cues from other children and adults.

Children need physical activity for their developing muscles and bones. Handheld games limit movement to fingers and thumbs. When typically active children become sedentary, they are at greater risk for obesity and sleep problems, and they have less time to play and practice social skills. The American Academy of Pediatrics (AAP, 2016) discourages media use, except for video chatting, for children younger than eighteen months. From ages eighteen to twenty-four months, parents may choose to introduce high-quality programming and apps together with their children, but young children shouldn't use the games alone. After age two, coviewing or coplaying may be appropriate for less than one hour each day. More appropriate activities include reading, talking, and playing together.

## Opting for Outside

Just stepping outside is an effective way to distract a crying baby. A fresh breeze and new sights and smells give people under three a way to refocus their attention. A ten-minute walk outside can lift everyone's spirits. Of course, safety is of primary concern when taking babies and toddlers outdoors. Get down on the child's level to check for hazards. Holes or gaps should be small enough to avoid trapping heads, hands, or fingers and to prevent young children from falling through. Check the playground each morning before the class goes outside to make sure nothing dangerous has developed since your last recess. Check for trash and debris that may have blown in or been dropped on the grounds. Look for broken tree limbs and cracks or breaks in the play equipment.

Some people believe that playgrounds exist to let the children run around and burn off some energy. Children do need to run and jump and use their large muscles, but that is only part of the story. Playgrounds and outdoor areas also provide opportunities to plan outdoor learning activities. Nature education has its own appeal to young children and is intrinsically motivating. Just being outside is rewarding. It makes us feel more relaxed and lowers our stress levels. Teachers and children get fresh air to breathe rather than breathing recirculated air, and sunshine offers vitamin D. It is worthwhile to find ways to incorporate the outdoors into our lesson plans every day that we possibly can.

An outdoor play area doesn't take a great deal of space if classes go outside at different times during the day. Create shade immediately with tent canopies or awnings, and plant bushes and fast-growing trees to provide natural shade in the future. Outdoor play materials do not need to be expensive. Pots, pans, and dishes can be found at garage sales, thrift stores, and resale shops; often, families will be happy to donate old items. Because these materials are inexpensive, they are fairly easily replaced when they become worn out. It's a good idea to have plenty of duplicates of favorite items, because toddlers and twos often like to do the same thing at the same time. Having lots of the popular materials will reduce conflicts.

If your area has experienced ice storms or high winds that have left behind lots of fallen trees, it's a great time to ask neighbors for unwanted branches that you can cut up. Use tree branches and trunks to create loose parts for your playground that will provide gross motor challenges for young children. They may want to climb on and over them. Large chunks of logs invite twos to collaborate with a friend to move them. Programs can create natural structures by securing poles and attaching burlap fabric that can transform a simple gravel path into a pathway to magical adventure.

## Challenging Classroom, Challenging Behaviors

- O  Sketch a map of your classroom floor plan.

- O  Place a star on the map in a specific area each time a concerning behavior occurs in that area. Consider posting the map on a cabinet door, so that each caregiver can add to it as needed.

- After a week, meet with your coteacher(s) and talk about where the star clusters are located. Discuss possible reasons for the issue in this/these area(s).

- Brainstorm ways to address the problem areas.

- Consider changes to the arrangement of furniture and daily schedule. Also consider how other parts of the classroom might be affecting these areas.

- Implement some changes.

- Observe for two weeks, adding stars to a clean copy of your floor plan. (Note: It's important to give any changes a couple of weeks so that you and the children can get used to them.)

- Meet with your coteacher(s) again, and compare the first and second maps. Have the concerning behaviors decreased? Have they increased? Use the information to decide whether the changes were worthwhile and whether more are needed.

- Repeat as needed.

# CHAPTER 7

## Developing the Environmental Mentor

Now that you have learned ways that child-care environments affect how babies, toddlers, and two-year-olds experience learning, let's take a look at your space. Consider ways you can provide experiences to help young children gain knowledge, practice new skills, and apply those ideas to different situations.

## The Classroom: Welcoming or Unwelcoming?

Reflect on your responses to the questions on page 35 in chapter 2 about the features that make a classroom inviting, interesting, and intriguing. Then use the following chart to evaluate classrooms you have visited and your own classroom.

- Think of classrooms you have visited that you found welcoming. What made them feel that way? What made you want to spend time there?

- Think of classrooms you have visited that you found unwelcoming. What made you feel that way? What made you want to leave?

- Use the chart to think about your own classroom. What areas are welcoming? What areas are not?

| Classroom Area | Welcoming? | Unwelcoming? |
|---|---|---|
| Stand in the doorway, and look around. | | |
| Examine the feeding and eating areas. | | |
| Look at the resting areas. | | |
| Listen. Do you hear music playing? Are there instruments for the children to explore and play? | | |
| Examine the block and manipulative areas. | | |
| Look at the book and literacy area. | | |
| Examine the cozy spaces. | | |
| Look at the dress-up and house areas. | | |
| Examine the art-exploration area. | | |
| Look at the lighting. What and where are the light sources? Are there windows? Is the lighting natural or artificial? Do you see mirrors? | | |

Use the information you gathered to think of ways to make your own spaces more welcoming.

- O What are the strengths of your classroom environment? What is working well?

- O What are you already working to improve?

- O How can you make your environment even better? If anything were possible, what do you wish you could improve?

Create a plan for making some improvements. Who might be able to help? Consider local mini grants, volunteers from the families you serve, and community groups.

- O What are your achievable steps?

- O What can you start right away?

- O What can you accomplish with a little more time?

- O What will the classroom look like when all of your dreams come true?

## Outdoor Play Spaces: Welcoming or Unwelcoming?

The features that make an indoor space inviting, interesting, and intriguing apply to outdoor spaces as well. Think of outdoor play spaces you have visited that you found welcoming. What made them feel that way? What made you want to spend time there? Think of outdoor play spaces you have visited that you found unwelcoming. What made you feel that way? What made you want to leave? Think about your own outdoor play spaces. What aspects are welcoming? What aspects are not?

- O Sketch a map of your playground.

- O Make copies for others who use the space.

- O Place a star on the map each time a concerning behavior occurs. Consider using a clipboard or tablet to make it easier to document events while outdoors.

- O After a week, meet with your colleagues and talk about where the star clusters occur. Consider why these spaces might be problematic.

- O Brainstorm ways to address the problem areas.

  - ■ Consider changes to the loose-parts arrangement.

- Think about the scheduled use of the space.

- Consider other parts of the playground that might affect the areas for infants, toddlers, and two-year-olds.

○ Implement some changes.

○ Observe for two weeks. On a fresh copy of the map, add stars for each concerning behavior.

○ Meet again and compare the first and second maps. Decide whether the changes were worthwhile and whether more changes are needed.</BL>

## Supportive or Unsupportive?

In chapter 1, we considered the elements needed to create a supportive indoor space. Using a copy of your classroom floor plan and the following chart, evaluate your classroom environment, arrangement, and materials.

| Questions to Consider | Yes | No | Changes Needed |
| --- | --- | --- | --- |
| Are the interest areas arranged into cozy smaller spaces? | | | |
| Are the children's families visible in photos or posters? | | | |
| Do the books, posters, toys, dolls, and dramatic-play props reflect the diversity in your classroom and in the world? | | | |
| Can you see and hear every child at all times? | | | |
| Are there enough comfortable places for adults to sit? | | | |
| How is lighting used to make the spaces more interesting? | | | |

| Questions to Consider | Yes | No | Changes Needed |
|---|---|---|---|
| Are mirrors placed at the children's eye level to promote understanding of their own emotions? | | | |
| Are interesting activities spread around the space so children aren't bunched up in the same spots? | | | |
| Are quiet activities away from noisy ones? | | | |
| Are messy activities strategically places for easier cleanup? | | | |
| Are there enough materials for each child to engage in interesting play? | | | |

## Considering the Daily Schedule

Use the following chart to create a list of the current daily activities in your classroom. Consider arranging the room to better accommodate these activities. Examine the daily routine to notice how often group and independent activities occur. Then consider changes you could make that would minimize transitions and give the children more choice.

## Daily Schedule

| Current Activities and Times | Current Groupings:<br><br>I = independent<br>SG = small group<br>M = most children | Possible Changes to Try |
|---|---|---|
| | | |
| | | |
| | | |
| | | |
| | | |
| | | |
| | | |
| | | |
| | | |
| | | |
| | | |
| | | |
| | | |
| | | |
| | | |
| | | |
| | | |
| | | |

# Examining Children's Activities and Interests

Use the following chart to take a time sample of the children's activities. Every half hour, place tally marks for the number of children in each area. At the bottom, count the total number of children in each area for the day.

| Time | Blocks | Library | Music | Eating/ Resting | Climbing/ Outside | Loose Parts | Pretending |
|------|--------|---------|-------|-----------------|-------------------|-------------|------------|
| 6:00 | | | | | | | |
| 6:30 | | | | | | | |
| 7:00 | | | | | | | |
| 7:30 | | | | | | | |
| 8:00 | | | | | | | |
| 8:30 | | | | | | | |
| 9:00 | | | | | | | |
| 9:30 | | | | | | | |
| 10:00 | | | | | | | |
| 10:30 | | | | | | | |
| 11:00 | | | | | | | |
| 11:30 | | | | | | | |
| 12:00 | | | | | | | |
| 12:30 | | | | | | | |
| 1:00 | | | | | | | |
| 1:30 | | | | | | | |
| 2:00 | | | | | | | |
| 2:30 | | | | | | | |
| 3:00 | | | | | | | |
| 3:30 | | | | | | | |
| 4:00 | | | | | | | |
| 4:30 | | | | | | | |
| 5:00 | | | | | | | |
| 5:30 | | | | | | | |
| 6:00 | | | | | | | |

# Learning Goals

Use the following chart to consider the specific learning goals for each child in your classroom. Consider each child's interests and think about ways to incorporate the child's personal preferences with learning goals to increase interest and motivation.

| _____'s Learning Goals and Interests | | |
|---|---|---|
| Child's Learning Goals | Child's Interests: What objects and activities does this person love? | Possible Connections between the Two |
| | | |
| | | |
| | | |
| | | |
| | | |
| | | |
| | | |
| | | |
| | | |
| | | |
| | | |
| | | |
| | | |
| | | |
| | | |

# CHAPTER 8

## Care for Caregivers

Caring for people under three is exhausting physical and mental work. It isn't enough to tell teachers that they should practice self-care in these stressful times; that's just one more thing on an already-too-full to-do list. As a teacher, please give yourself permission to be imperfect. We make a thousand decisions a day. They won't all be the right decisions, but each mistake is also an opportunity to reflect on our choices and do things differently the next time.

Although healthier habits, including exercise, nutrition, positive self-talk, and mindfulness, do help reduce stress, we also need to work toward public awareness of the importance of this work and appropriate compensation. Teachers deserve the admiration and respect that our profession was once given in this country and that continues to be afforded in other countries around the world, as well as adequate compensation. Ours is the profession that makes all other professions possible. While the joy of working with children is rewarding, it does not pay the bills. We can all advocate for child-care providers in big and small ways: speaking to one person, to small groups, and even before Congress.

## Magical Ordinary Days

Each child has to make sense of the events and surroundings in her unique lifeworld. Many young children begin their day in their own homes, immersed in familiar routines. Their senses are flooded with comforting sights, smells, and predictable interactions. When they go to school, they have to readjust their expectations to a new caregiver, whose day may be going according to plan or may have veered off course already. Both children and adults are affected by everything that happens inside and outside the classroom. Coffee and milk get spilled, shoes get lost, the best intentions can go awry. Early childhood professionals must act in ways that are appropriate despite their own moods and must adjust their feelings to fit the moods of each child, every day. That can be exhausting.

The ordinary moments that children experience each day can actually be magical from the child's point of view. A new day can be filled with exciting discoveries, new thoughts, and fresh ideas. A baby suddenly notices his hands and become mesmerized by them. Life will never the same once he has mastered the art of grasping a Cheerio! A toddler finds a wooden yardstick and lifts it overhead in triumph! A two-year-old scales a small boulder in the park and stands on the summit, turning to make sure that her friends have witnessed this achievement! For children, the little things are the big things.

One goal of learning is to have a new thought—a thought that you hadn't ever thought of before. As you reflect on your classroom environment, consider the opportunities it presents for children and adults to have new thoughts. Intentionally

planned learning environments inspire children to think new thoughts and to have wonderful ideas of their own. Through the arrangement of space, careful selection of materials, and consideration for beauty that appeals to all of our senses, we can plan for joyful, authentic learning. People under three have a lot to process in their world. Classrooms should be calming, comforting places where children feel safe and secure and inspired to learn.

## Mirrors and Windows

Emily Style first introduced "mirrors and windows" as a way to think about perspectives in literature. A mirror allows you to see yourself and your own culture reflected in a story. A window lets you peer into someone else's experience. We can adapt this concept of mirrors and windows as a way to think about the universal needs of infants, toddlers, and twos. Mirrors let us reflect on our current practices. The children we serve are alike, yet each child is unique. All children need love, acceptance, respect, and intellectual challenges. Mirrors allow us to reflect on who we are as teachers and where we have come from. Windows allow us to have vision for the future. What possibilities would we imagine if no barriers existed? Windows allow us to see the world beyond our current experiences. They let in the light to illuminate our future growth.

## Contradictions

Observation is the art of knowing when to intervene. Young children need security and independence. We need to give them space to explore and try new ideas; yet, we must remain close at hand in case they truly need us. We should not ignore children's conflicts or indications that they need comfort but should stay alert to assist as needed. Supervise by sight and sound at all times, but do not hover over them. Our presence and willingness to respond when needed provides the security that babies need to have the confidence to explore. We are strengthening neural pathways. The more babies use their brains to make cognitive connections, the more efficiently their brains function. The opposite is also true; unused pathways will be pruned away.

With practice, we hone our observation skills for this detective work. By watching each baby to see what they are telling us, we learn all that we need to know to meet their needs. Babies are theorists, testing their ideas. Teachers are researchers as they seek to improve their understanding by paying careful attention. Intentional teachers take their cues from people under three in playing, planning lessons, and collaborating with families. Respectful approaches to teaching and learning are reflected in the design of the space and consideration for the needs of children and their families. Young children have a limitless capacity to learn.

## From Grit to Pearls

Beautiful jewelry is usually created from rare crystals and precious metals, but one gem is formed through biological processes. When an irritant (not usually a grain of sand, as you might have been told) enters a mussel, clam, or oyster, the animal responds by building up layer upon layer of nacre, a strong, iridescent outer coating. In the same way, teachers respond to challenges by adding to their skills and understanding layer upon layer until a thing of great strength and beauty results. Diamonds, rubies, and sapphires are cut and polished from the outside by craftspeople to reveal their beauty, but pearls are formed from the inside out. The longer they are built up, the stronger and more valuable they become. Grit is the passion and perseverance that transforms teachers into irreplaceable pearls. Know your value and shine on.

◆ ◆ ◆

# Reflecting Back and Looking Forward

## Mirrors

- Reflect on how and why things are the way they currently are.

- Think about your current classroom learning environment.

## Windows

- Think about how you hope things will be in the future.

- Think about approaches, ideas, and strategies you want to try.

# References and Recommended Reading

American Academy of Pediatrics. 2016. "Media Use in School-Aged Children and Adolescents." *Pediatrics* 138(5): e20162592. https://doi.org/10.1542/peds.2016-2592

Barragan, Rodolfo, Rechele Brooks, and Andrew Meltzoff. 2020. "Altruistic Food Sharing Behavior by Human Infants after a Hunger Manipulation." *Scientific Reports* 10:1785. https://doi.org/10.1038/s41598-020-58645-9

Brazelton, T. Berry, and Kevin Nugent. 2011. *Neonatal Behavioral Assessment Scale*. 4th ed. London, UK: Mac Keith Press.

Carle, Eric. 2011. *Eric Carle, Picture Writer: The Art of the Picture Book*. Kate Geis, director.

Colker, Laura J., and Derry Koralek. 2020. "Learned Optimism: A Critical Skill for Teaching and Learning." Community Playthings. https://www.communityplaythings.com/resources/articles/2020/learned-optimism

Duncan, Sandra. 2011. "Breaking the Code: Changing Our Thinking about Children's Environments." *Exchange* 33(4).

Eckhart, Kim. 2020. "Altruistic Babies? Study Shows Infants Are Willing to Give Up Food, Help Others." *UW News*, February 4. https://www.washington.edu/news/2020/02/04/altruistic-babies-study-shows-infants-are-willing-to-give-up-food-help-others/

Forman, George, and Ellen Hall. 2005. "Wondering with Children: The Importance of Observation in Early Education." *Early Childhood Research and Practice* 7(2).

Hartshorne, Joshua, Joshua Tenenbaum, and Steven Pinker. 2018. "A Critical Period for Second-Language Acquisition: Evidence from 2/3 Million English Speakers." *Cognition* 177: 263–277.

Hu, Tian-Yi, Jingyu Li, Huiyan Jia, and Xiaofei Xie. 2016. "Helping Others, Warming Yourself: Altruistic Behaviors Increase Warmth Feelings of the Ambient Environment." *Frontiers in Psychology* 7:1349. https://doi.org/10.3389/fpsyg.2016.01349

Kamenetz, Anya. 2018. "5 Proven Benefits of Play." nprEd. https://www.npr.org/sections/ed/2018/08/31/642567651/5-proven-benefits-of-play

Lally, Ron. 2000. "The Importance of Social and Emotional Attachment." *Ensuring Quality and Accountability through Leadership: A User's Guide*. Washington, DC: Head Start Bureau, Administration on Children, Youth, and Families, Administration for Children and Families, US Department of Health and Human Services.

Legendre, Alain. 1995. "The Effects of Environmentally Modulated Visual Accessibility to Caregivers on Early Peer Interactions." *International Journal of Behavioral Development* 18(2): 297–313.

Lew-Williams, Casey. 2016. "Forget Flashcards, Play With Sticks. An Expert Explains How Children Learn." *World Economic Forum,* October 3. https://www.weforum.org/agenda/2016/10/forget-flashcards-play-with-sticks-an-expert-explains-how-children-learn/

Park, Alice. 2015. "This Is a Baby's Brain on Pain." *Time* April 21. https://time.com/3827167/this-is-a-babys-brain-on-pain/

Perry, Bruce D. n.d. "Creating an Emotionally Safe Classroom." Scholastic. https://www.scholastic.com/teachers/articles/teaching-content/creating-emotionally-safe-classroom/

Perry, Bruce D. n.d. "Curiosity: The Fuel of Development." Scholastic. https://www.scholastic.com/teachers/articles/teaching-content/emotional-development-curiosity-fuel-development/

Pica, Rae. 2018. "In Defense of Active Learning." Community Playthings. https://www.communityplaythings.com/resources/articles/2018/In-Defense-of-Active-Learning

Pratt, Michelle. 2014. "Environments that Speak to Children." *Exchange* 36(5). https://www.childcareexchange.com/article/environments-that-speak-to-children/5021928/

Puura, Kaija, Elmarie Malek, and Astrid Berg. 2018. "Integrating Infant Mental Health at Primary Health Care Level." *Perspectives in Infant Mental Health* 26(2-3): 4-6.

Stephens, Karen. 2015. "Ceiling Fascinations: Good Reasons to Look Up!" *Exchange* 37(2).

Sullivan, Meg. 2016. "Your Brain Might Be Hard-Wired for Altruism." UCLA Newsroom: Health + Behavior, March 18. https://newsroom.ucla.edu/releases/your-brain-might-be-hard-wired-for-altruism

Vasandani, Sony. 2015. "Creating Environments that Reduce Children's Stress." *Exchange* 37(6): 40 -43.

Wadsworth, Olive. 1962. *Over in the Meadow.* New York: Wonder Books.

Walsh, Theadora. 2020. "In Rhoda Kellogg's World, Every Child Is an Artist." KQED, February 10. https://www.kqed.org/arts/13874655/rhoda-kellogg-sfac-city-hall

Warneken, Felix, and Michael Tomasello. 2006. "Altruistic Helping in Human Infants and Young Chimpanzees." *Science* 311(5765): 1301–1303

Wyont, Wanda. 2018. "Shape Young Minds Learn Through Sensory Environments --Learn How, It's Easy!" Fractus Learning. https://www.fractuslearning.com/sensory-environment-brain-development/.

# Index